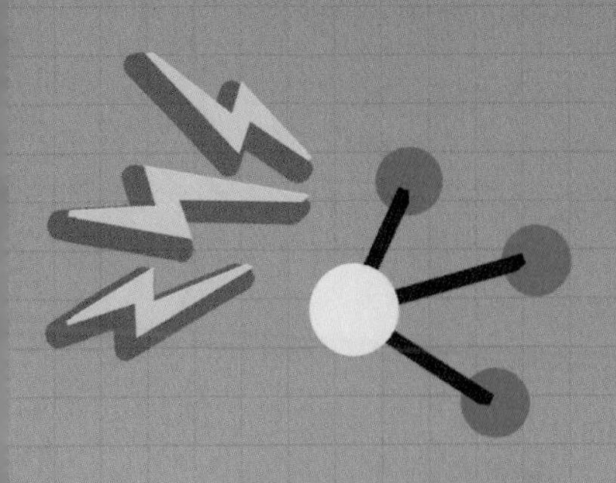

THE BIG BOOK OF SPEEDY SCIENCE

THE BIG BOOK OF SPEEDY SCIENCE

Written by Anna Claybourne

Illustrated by Kimberley Scott
and Venetia Dean

Make it bang!

Make it zoom!

SWING

WHOOOOSH

ZOOOM!

Make it glow!

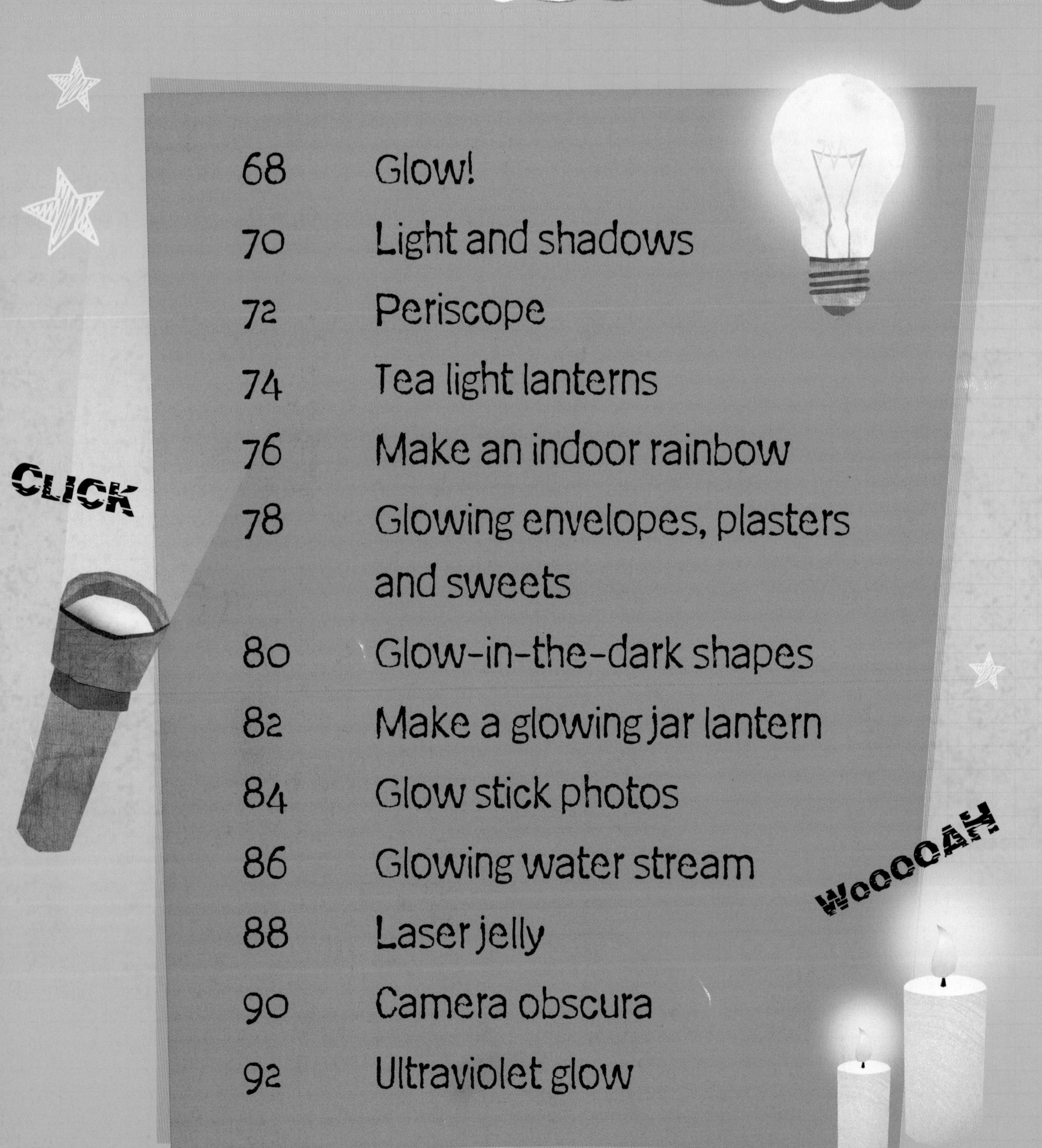

Make it change!

YUM, YUM!

SIZZLE

Make it splash!

DRIP, DRIP

SPLOSH

Make it grow!

YUM, YUM!

JUICY!

GROWING

Make it Bang!

BANG!!!

What makes things go BANG? Or crash, clatter, squeak, creak, hoot or any other sound? The answer is movement. Sound is a kind of energy that comes from things moving and shaking quickly to and fro – also known as vibrating.

WHIZZZZ

LIKE WHAT?

Things vibrate in different ways to make all kinds of sounds.

BANG! If you bang a door shut, it vibrates suddenly, making a loud, short noise.

CRASH! Hitting a cymbal makes the metal vibrate with a loud crashing sound.

Laaaaaa! When you sing or talk, you blow air through stringy bits of muscle in your throat, and they vibrate.

INTO YOUR EARS

Of course, we only know what all these sounds are like because we can hear them. They spread out through the air and go into our ears, which are specially built to detect them. Hearing is amazingly useful – it helps us talk to each other, send long-distance messages, spot danger, and enjoy TV, films and music.

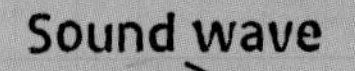

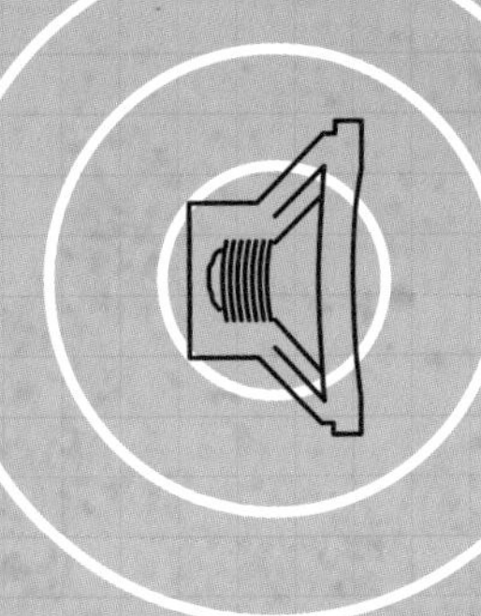

BEING A SCIENTIST

This book is packed full of fun experiments to try with bangs, crashes and other sounds, to help you find out how sounds work. To get the best results, here are a few sound science tips:

1. Set up your experiments according to the instructions and watch carefully to see what happens.
2. To be like a real scientist, write down your results in a notebook.
3. Scientists often do experiments several times over, to check they always work the same way.

See a bang

Everything that makes a sound is moving, but you can't always see the vibrations that make sound. This experiment makes it a bit easier to spot them!

YOU WILL NEED

1) An empty food container
2) Clingfilm or a plastic bag
3) Long elastic bands
4) A pencil or wooden spoon
5) Rice grains

Here's What to Do...

1. Remove the lid from your food container.

2. Stretch a large piece of the plastic bag or clingfilm tightly around the container, and hold it in place with elastic bands.

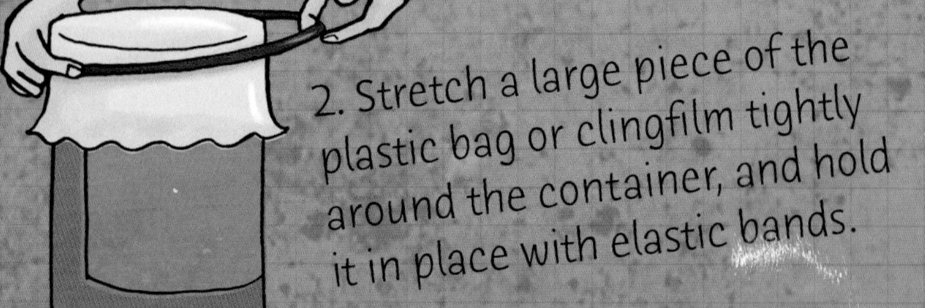

3. Sprinkle a pinch of rice onto the surface of your 'drum'.

4. Bang the drum gently with a pencil or wooden spoon.

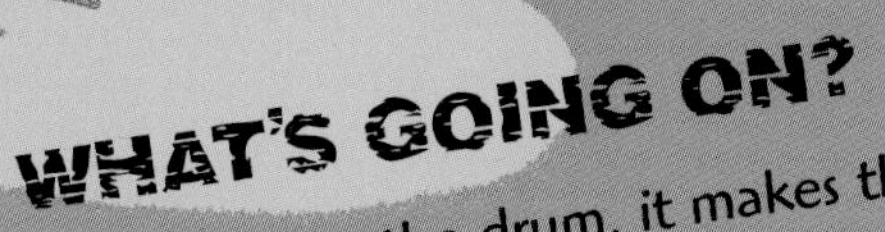

WHAT'S GOING ON?

When you hit the drum, it makes the plastic skin vibrate very quickly up and down. It's hard to see, because the vibrations are quite small and fast. But if there are rice grains sitting on top, the vibrations make them jump up and down, showing you what's happening.

TROUBLESHOOTER

The plastic should be very tight and smooth. You may need two people to put it on – one to hold it while the other fixes it in place.

WHAT NEXT?

Do the rice grains behave differently if you put them near the edge or right in the middle?

Try making a loud noise just above the drum without touching it (shout, clap or bang things together) – can you make the rice grains jump? Why does this happen?

Bang, twang, pop

Try making some loud and peculiar noises using some of the everyday objects around you. See if you can work out why they sound different from each other.

Here's What to Do...

YOU WILL NEED

1) Wooden blocks, bricks or chopping boards
2) A ruler
3) A balloon
4) A coin with lots of sides (a screw nut with six sides also works)

1. Clap your hands, stamp your feet, or bang two blocks of wood together.

2. Put your finger in your mouth, close it tightly, blow hard, then pop your finger out sideways.

3. Hold a ruler firmly over the edge of a table, and twang the free end.

4. Put a multi-sided coin inside a balloon, blow it up and tie it, then twirl it around to make the coin roll fast around the inside.

WHAT'S GOING ON?

All these activities involve hitting or somehow moving an object to make it vibrate. The sound the object makes depends on how it moves, and what it is made of. Springy or rubbery objects such as the ruler and the balloon skin tend to make more twangy, long-lasting sounds, as they bounce to and fro. Hard, rigid objects such as wooden blocks stop vibrating more quickly, and make short, sharp sounds.

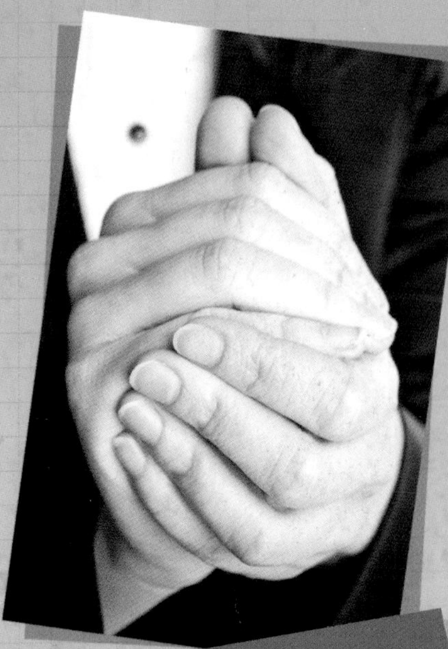

Can you make a hooting owl sound with your hands? Cup them together, with a gap between your thumbs, and blow gently across the gap.

DID YOU KNOW?

If there is air inside a vibrating object, the air will vibrate too, adding to the sound.

WHAT NEXT?

Write down descriptions of each sound – are they high or low, loud or quiet, spooky, funny or strange?

How a bang travels

Why can we hear sound? Because it travels from the moving object to our ears, in the form of sound waves. This experiment shows how sound waves work.

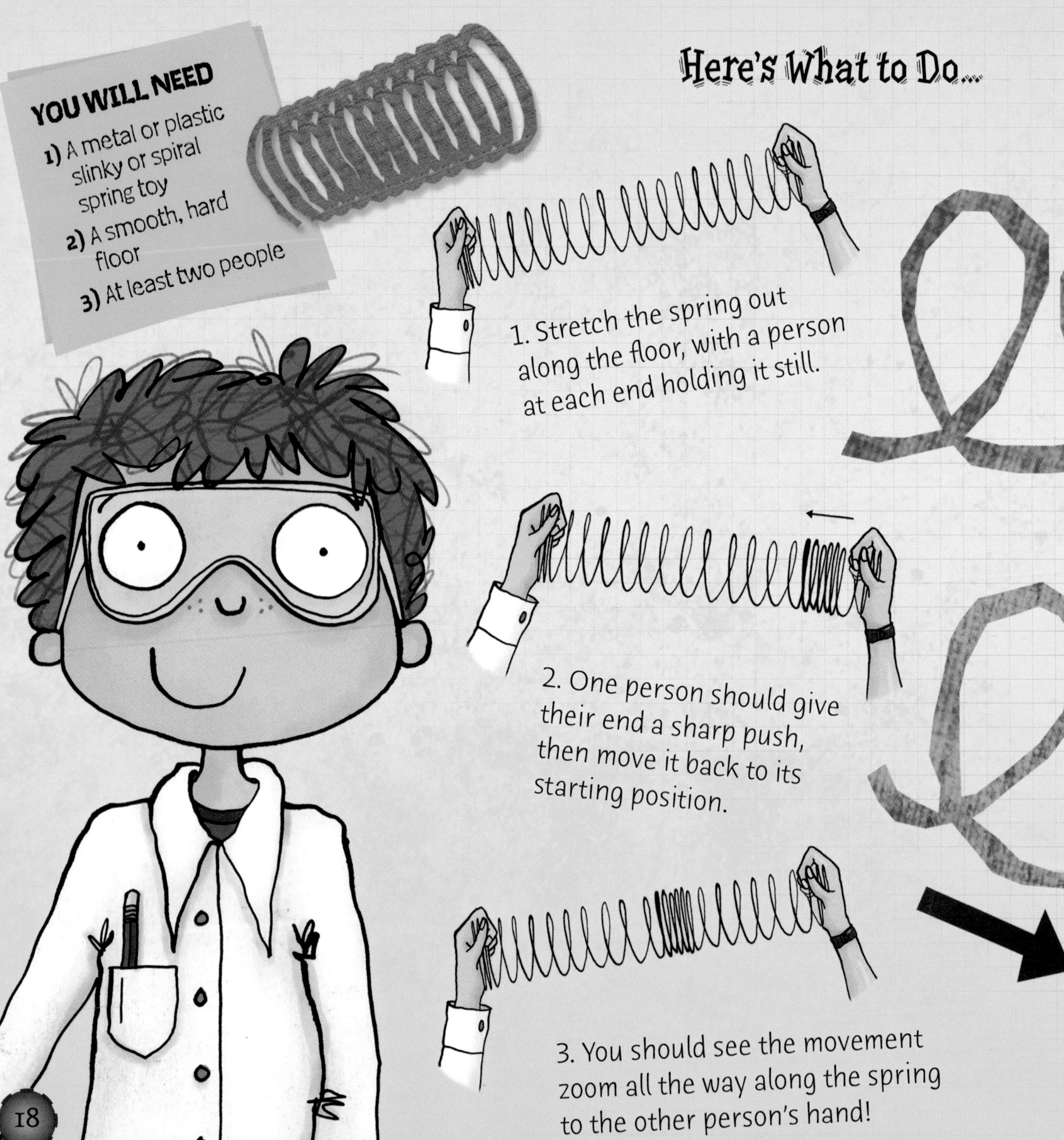

YOU WILL NEED

1) A metal or plastic slinky or spiral spring toy
2) A smooth, hard floor
3) At least two people

Here's What to Do...

1. Stretch the spring out along the floor, with a person at each end holding it still.

2. One person should give their end a sharp push, then move it back to its starting position.

3. You should see the movement zoom all the way along the spring to the other person's hand!

WHAT'S GOING ON?

When you push the end of the spring, the first coil pushes the next coil, which pushes the next one, and so on. In this way the energy of the push moves right along the spring.

TROUBLESHOOTER

The spring needs to be spread out, but not pulled too tight; experiment to find the best amount of stretch.

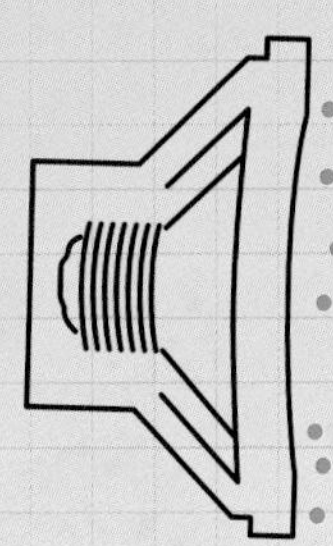

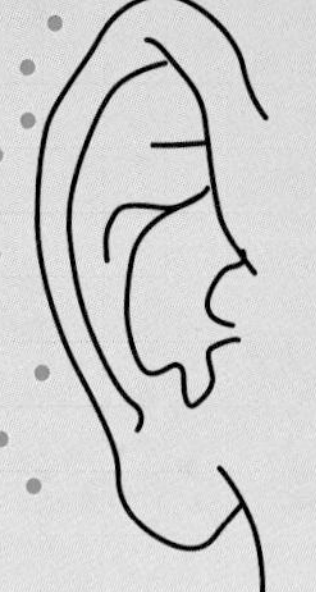

Sound waves in air work the same way. When something vibrates, it pushes against the tiny molecules in the air around it, making them vibrate too. They push the molecules next to them, and they push the molecules next to them, and so on.

BOUNCING BACK

An echo is a sound wave that has bounced off a surface. If you can tape one end of your spring to a wall, you may be able to recreate this, too.

WHAT NEXT?

Can you send a series of waves down your slinky, one following another?

Can you recreate how a sound wave travels using a line of people?

The speed of a bang

You hit a drum or shut a door, and you hear a sound – BANG! It seems as if it happens straight away. But actually it takes time for sound to travel to your ears. So how fast does it go?

YOU WILL NEED

1) A tape measure or measuring wheel
2) Two bin lids, pan lids or cymbals
3) A stopwatch
4) A pen and paper
5) A calculator
6) At least two people

Here's What to Do...

1. Measure out a distance of 250 metres (m) on a flat playing field, park or beach.

2. One person should stand 250 m away from the other, and bang the lids or cymbals together.

3. The other person should start the timer when they see the bang happening, and stop it when they hear the bang. You'll need to react quickly!

4. Write down how long the bang takes to travel 250 m. From this you can calculate the speed of sound (see What's Going On?).

WHAT'S GOING ON?

When the lids bang, the sound starts to spread out through the air. You see it happen almost immediately, as the speed of light is very, very fast. But sound is much slower. If you are 250 m away, it should take about 0.7 seconds to reach you.

To find the speed of sound in metres per second, divide 250 by your result.

For example, 250 divided by 0.73 = about 342 metres per second.

This is the same as about 1,235 kilometres per hour (km/h) or 768 miles per hour (mph) – as fast as a very fast jet plane. Zoom!

TROUBLESHOOTER

You need a calm day – avoid noisy wind and rain!

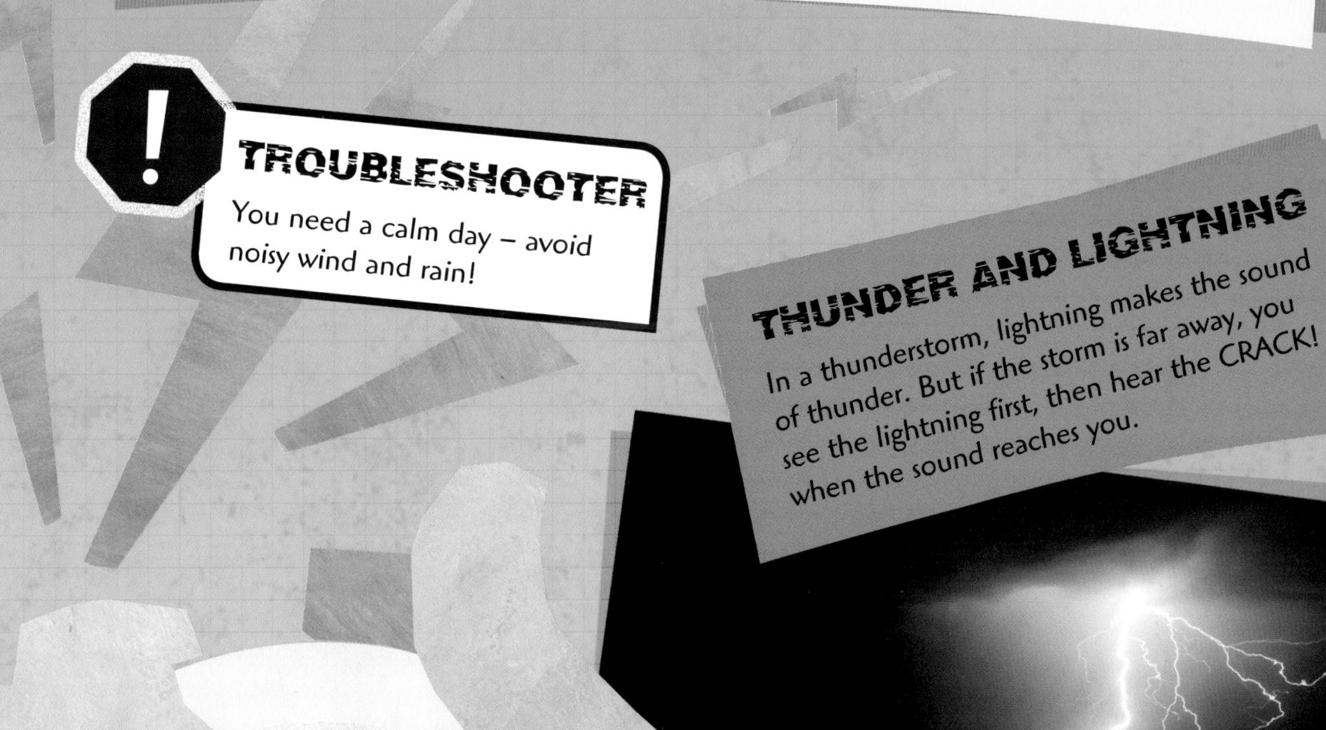

THUNDER AND LIGHTNING

In a thunderstorm, lightning makes the sound of thunder. But if the storm is far away, you see the lightning first, then hear the CRACK! when the sound reaches you.

WHAT NEXT?

Do the experiment several times to get a good average measurement.

Can you do it over an even bigger distance?

Bangs and whispers

Why are some sounds loud and others quiet? Try making sounds of different volumes and see if you can work out what's happening.

YOU WILL NEED

1) A drum and drumstick, or a pan and a wooden spoon
2) Musical instruments, if you have any
3) Everyday objects
4) A pen and paper

Here's What to Do...

1. Try making loud and quiet bangs on your drum or pan.

2. Try making loud and quiet sounds on a musical instrument or by singing.

3. Try clapping, rubbing objects together, or rattling a box with something inside.

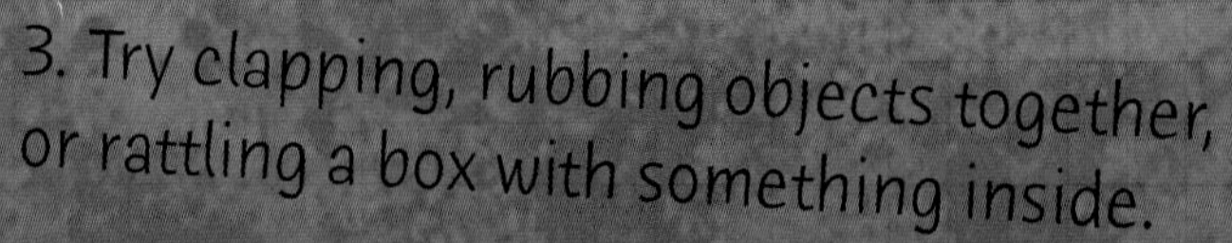

4. Write down what you have to do to make sound louder in each experiment.

WHAT'S GOING ON?

Whatever you're using to make a sound, making it louder always involves the same thing. Did you notice what it was? Sound is a form of energy, and louder sounds carry more energy, as they involve stronger vibrations. So to make louder sounds, you have to put more energy in. That means hitting, blowing or shaking harder. Put in a lot less energy, and you get a really quiet sound instead.

SOUND SCALE

Scientists measure how loud sounds are using the decibel or dB scale. Very quiet sounds, like rustling leaves, measure about 20 dB. Super-loud sounds like a jet taking off are around 140 dB.

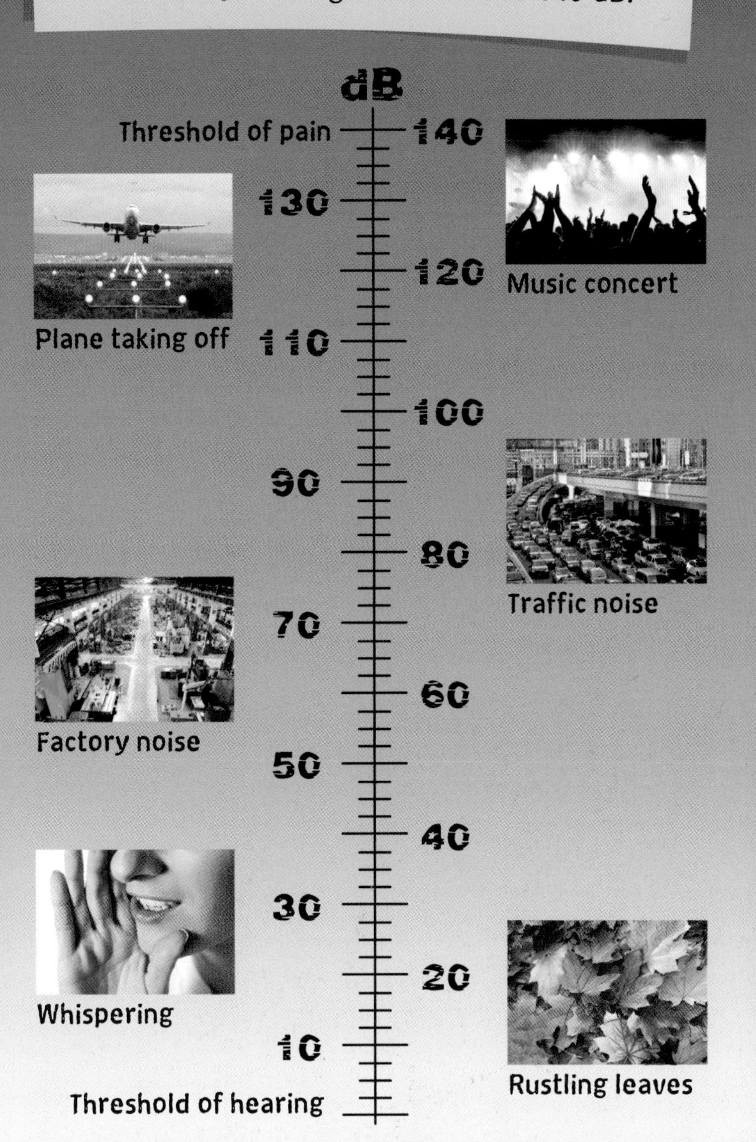

WHAT NEXT?

Experiment with the plastic drum skin and rice grains from page 14. Do the rice grains behave differently when you bang the drum skin harder?

Whispering is another way to be quiet, but to do this, you stop your voice from making a sound, and just use your breath. How quietly can you talk without whispering?

The Screaming cup

How can you make a cup shriek and squawk like a parrot? It might seem pretty unlikely, but here's how to do it...

WHAT'S GOING ON?

As your fingers slip down the thread in sudden jerks and jumps, they make it vibrate. The vibrations are small and you would normally hardly hear anything. But as the thread is connected to the cup, it makes the cup vibrate too, along with the air inside it. This makes a louder sound... ...which sounds a bit like a squawking parrot!

Squawk!

PAPER CUP PHONE CALL

A paper cup telephone works in the same way. You use a long piece of string to join two cups together, then stretch it tight. When you speak into one cup, the vibrations travel along the string and into the other cup, making it sound as if the other person is right next to you!

AMPLIFICATION

Making sounds louder is called amplifying them.

TROUBLESHOOTER

If it doesn't work, try gripping the thread with a damp paper towel.

WHAT NEXT?

What happens if you put the cup to your ear and tap the bottom of it?

Try cutting the bottom off a paper cup and speaking through it.

High and low

How high or low a sound is, is called its pitch. Every sound has a pitch, and musical instruments and voices can change their pitch. How do they do it?

WHAT'S GOING ON?

With both these experiments, you are changing the pitch of a sound. You are actually doing this by making the vibrations faster or slower. When there's less air in the bottle, it makes shorter and faster vibrations, and a higher-pitched sound. When the elastic band is shorter, it vibrates to and fro faster, and its pitch is higher.

HOW MANY HERTZ?

Pitch is measured by the number of vibrations per second, also called Hertz, or Hz. For example, the top string on a guitar is about 330 Hz, meaning it vibrates 330 times every second – quite fast!

WHAT NEXT?

You can blow across the top of the bottles to make a different sound – but is it the same pitch?

If you have several bottles the same size and shape, you can use different amounts of water to 'tune' them to different notes, and make a bottle xylophone. What tunes can you play?

The sounds of speech

You always have one musical instrument with you – your voice! Find out how you make it go up and down, and why.

YOU WILL NEED

Not much! Your voice and your hands.

Here's What to Do...

1. Put your fingers gently on your throat, like this.

2. Sing loudly, starting very low, and moving up to a high note, then back down.

3. Now change between singing a note, and blowing while making no sound.

WHAT'S GOING ON?

Your voice is made by two bands of muscle in your throat called vocal cords or vocal folds. To make your voice higher, they stretch, so that they are tighter and vibrate faster. When you sing low, they are looser and vibrate more slowly. Parts of your throat have to move around to change their position, and you can feel this with your hand.

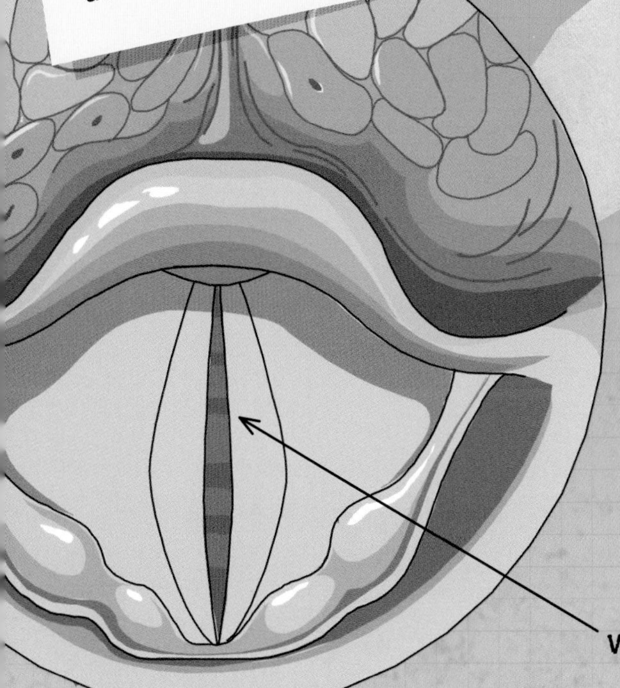

Vocal cords together make a sound.

TROUBLESHOOTER

You might need to move your hand around a bit at first to find the best position.

You can also move your vocal cords apart so that they don't vibrate at all. This happens when you blow, whisper or breathe normally. When they're together, you can feel the vibrations, but when they are apart, the vibrations stop.

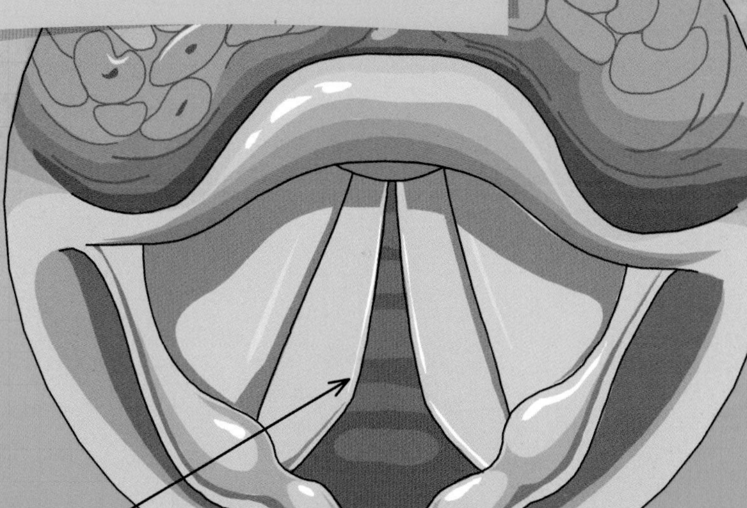

Vocal cords apart for breathing.

WHAT NEXT?

Think about what pitch is for – why is it useful for our voices to go up and down?

Try speaking without changing pitch at all. It's hard!

Try saying one word, such as 'yes', 'no' or 'OK', but using pitch to give it different meanings – for example try to sound keen, bored or rude. See if other people understand you!

Solid sounds

Sounds travel differently through solid objects, such as spoons, string and fingers than they do through the air. Find out what happens with this dangling, jangling spoon experiment!

YOU WILL NEED

1) String
2) A metal spoon
3) A table or other hard object

Here's What to Do...

1. Tie a 30-cm long piece of string to the handle of a metal spoon.

2. Wrap the other end of the string around your finger a few times, and bang the spoon gently against a table to make a ringing noise.

3. Now do the same thing again, but with the finger with the string around it pressed against your ear. Does it sound any different?

WHAT'S GOING ON?

When the sound just travels from the spoon through the air to your ears, it's quieter. When it travels along the spoon, the string and your finger into your ear, it sounds louder and a bit clearer. Solid things actually carry sounds better and faster than air does.

There's a simple reason for this – solids contain more molecules than air, and they're more tightly packed together. This means sound vibrations pass from one molecule to the next more easily and quickly in solids.

SAFETY WARNING

Press your finger gently against your ear, but DON'T stick it right inside – it's not very good for you.

Solid

Liquid

Gas

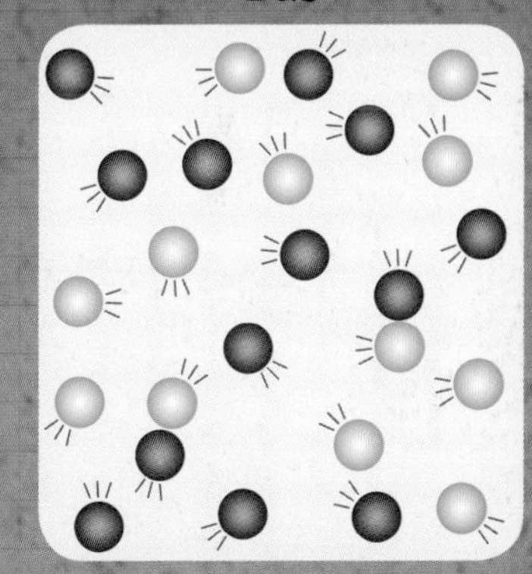

You could try this experiment with other solid objects, too, such as a ruler or a plastic cup. What works best?

FEELING FOR SOUNDS

Deaf people can sometimes get a better sense of sounds by touching the vibrating object to pick up the sound vibrations. Percussion player Evelyn Glennie, for example, performs with bare feet to help her sense vibrations through the ground.

WHAT NEXT?

What happens if you put your ears under the water in the bath while the tap is running? Sound also travels better through liquids than in air, as liquids have more molecules.

Stop that banging

Sometimes, you want to stop sound and keep it quiet. In fact, sometimes loud noises can be a problem. So what's the best way to block out sounds?

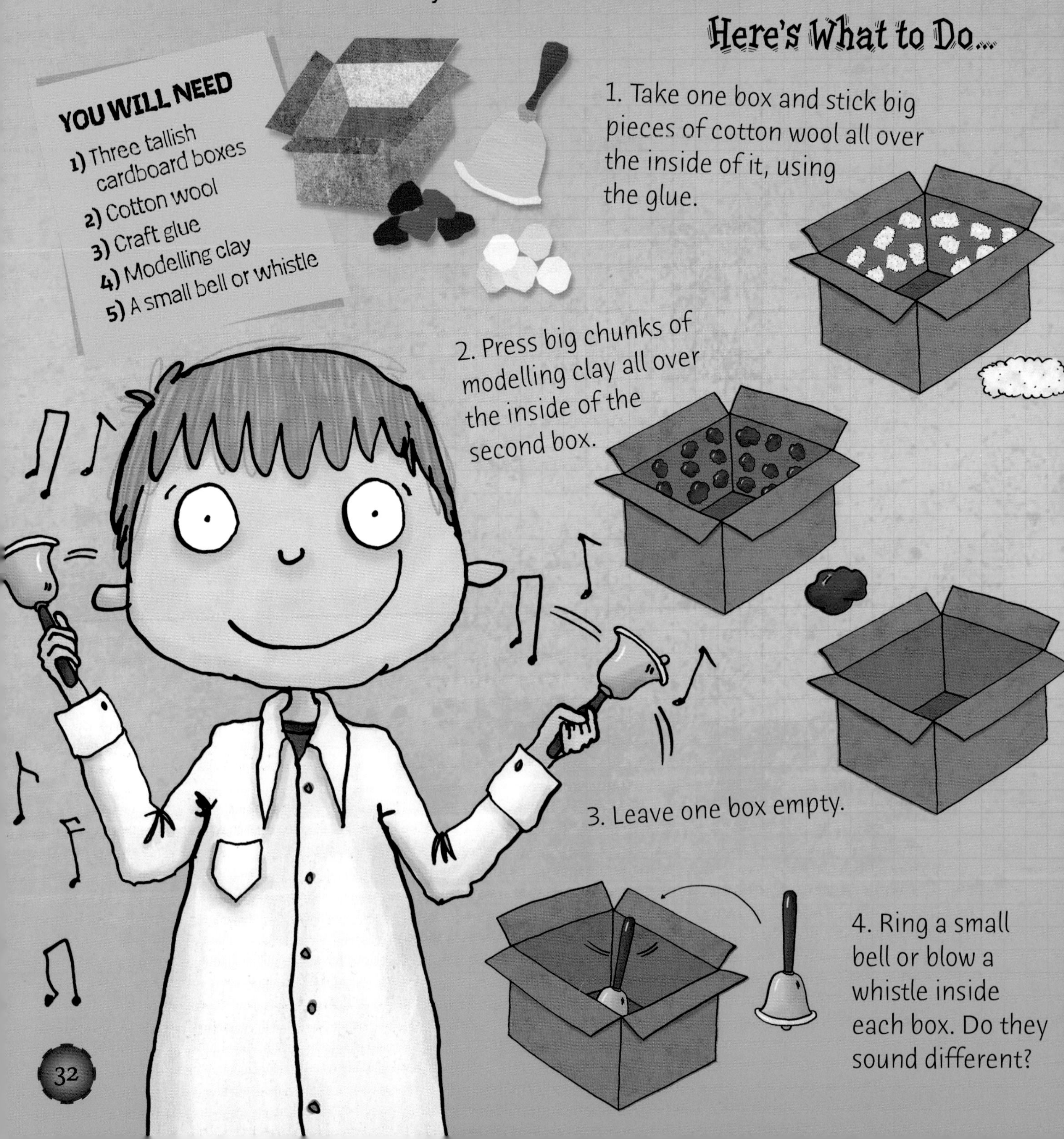

YOU WILL NEED

1) Three tallish cardboard boxes
2) Cotton wool
3) Craft glue
4) Modelling clay
5) A small bell or whistle

Here's What to Do...

1. Take one box and stick big pieces of cotton wool all over the inside of it, using the glue.

2. Press big chunks of modelling clay all over the inside of the second box.

3. Leave one box empty.

4. Ring a small bell or blow a whistle inside each box. Do they sound different?

WHAT'S GOING ON?

Sound bounces and echoes off some surfaces, but gets absorbed or soaked up by others. The softer and woollier the surface, the better it is at soaking up sound and making it seem quieter. We use this muffling effect for soundproofing – trying to stop unwanted sounds from spreading.

TROUBLESHOOTER

For it to work well the boxes should all be the same size.

BLOCK YOUR EARS!

Really loud sounds can damage your hearing, so people who work with loud noises need to protect their ears. Ear defenders like these block out sound with several layers of foam, wool or rubber.

Earplugs, made of squishy foam-like material, fit just inside the ears.

Ear defenders sit over the top of your ears to block out sound.

WHAT NEXT?

What makes the best sound insulation? Try other materials too, such as cardboard, felt, tissue paper or a woolly sock.

When would sound insulation be useful? Think about where you would put it to keep a bedroom quiet at night, or stop the sounds of music escaping from a recording studio.

find the bang

Can you tell which direction a sound is coming from? If you have two ears you can, and often do! How is that possible?

YOU WILL NEED

1) A scarf or eye mask to use as a blindfold
2) A chair
3) A group of at least four people

Here's What to Do...

1. One person should put on the blindfold and sit in the chair.

2. The others should stand in a ring around the chair, and take turns to make a noise.

3. The listener should try to point to where each noise is coming from.

WHAT'S GOING ON?

We use the fact that we have two ears to detect the direction of sounds. As sound takes time to travel, it reaches your ears at very slightly different times. You don't notice this, but your brain can tell! It uses the information to help it work out where sounds are coming from.

The outer part of your ear helps too. Its shape reflects sounds into your ear in different patterns depending on what direction they come from. Again, your brain can spot these tiny differences.

SATELLITE EARS

The sticking-out part of your ear, called the pinna, works a bit like a satellite dish to catch sounds and bounce them into your ears. It also protects your earhole from wind, rain and dirt!

WHAT NEXT?

What happens if the person in the chair covers up one of their ears? Does the task become harder?

Take turns so that everyone has a go on the chair. Are some people better than others at hearing where sounds come from?

How musical are you?

Some people find it easy to listen to and remember tunes, while others find it almost impossible. Test yourself and your friends!

YOU WILL NEED

1) A piano, xylophone or electronic keyboard
2) A scarf or eye mask to use as a blindfold

Here's What to Do...

1. The person being tested should put on the blindfold and face away from the keyboard.

2. Play two different notes on the keyboard, fairly close together, one after the other.

3. Ask the listener if they know whether the notes have moved up or down in pitch.

4. If they get that right, ask them how many keys apart the notes were.

WHAT'S GOING ON?

The ability to hear tunes and different notes is partly in your genes, meaning you are born with it. It can also be affected by how much you have learned about music. However, a few people – around 4 out of every 100 – simply cannot do it, however hard they try! Their brains simply don't work that way.

TROUBLESHOOTER

Make sure the blindfold doesn't cover the person's ears!

PERFECT PITCH

Some people have an ability called perfect pitch, which means they can actually name a particular note when they hear it.

WHAT'S THAT RACKET?

There are a few people who cannot understand musical sounds at all. To them, music just sounds like a jumble of noises, and some even find it upsetting. This condition is called amusia.

WHAT NEXT?

Test to see if anyone can sing the exact notes they have heard. If they can manage two notes easily, see if they can sing three, four or five in a row.

Make it Zoom!

Zoooooom!

What makes things zoom? What makes them whizz, slide, fall, crash or bump? The answer is forces. A force is a push or a pull that can make things move, stop or change shape.

GULP! Muscles in your throat squeeze hard to push food down into your stomach.

PLOP! If you throw a stone in a pond, your hand pushes it up, then gravity pulls it into the water.

LIKE WHAT?

There are forces at work all the time, all around you (and even inside you), making things happen. In fact, without these forces, nothing could happen at all!

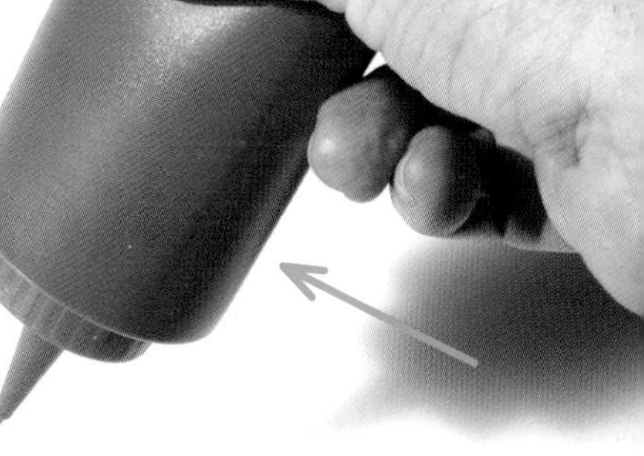

SQUEEEZE! You force paint out of a tube by squishing the sides.

BOING! To jump on a trampoline, you push upwards with your legs.

Your legs push you up

Gravity pulls you down

WHEEEEE! The force of gravity pulls you down a slide, or along a zipline.

VROOM! Engines burn fuel and turn wheels or propellers to make cars, buses and planes move.

WHOOOSH!

BEING A SCIENTIST

This book is full of exciting zooming, flying, sliding and squirting experiments to help you find out more about how forces work. When you're doing science experiments, be like a real scientist and remember these science tips:

1. Follow the instructions and always watch carefully to see what happens.
2. Write down your results in a notebook so you don't forget them.
3. Scientists often do experiments several times, to check they always work the same way.

Zooming cars

Use forces to make toy cars zoom, crash, jump and fly!

YOU WILL NEED

1) Several toy cars
2) Large, thin books or sheets of thick card
3) Toy bricks or small books
4) A large, hard floor space

Here's What to Do...

1. Push a car to see how far you can make it go.

2. Make a slope using card or a book, like this. Does it make the cars go? How?

3. Line up two cars opposite each other and crash them together.

4. Can you make a car do a daredevil leap over a row of other cars, then land safely?

WHAT'S GOING ON?

Making a car move in different ways uses different forces. You push a car using your hand. If you push it harder, you use more force, and it goes further.

If a car is at the top of a slope, the Earth's gravity pulls it down. Gravity is a pulling force between objects. The Earth's gravity is strong because the Earth has so much mass (it is so big and heavy).

When two cars crash, they push against each other. The pushes cancel each other out, stopping their movement.

TROUBLESHOOTER

Push cars as straight as possible to stop them from skidding. If you have special toy car tracks, you can use them to set up slopes, crashes and jumps, too.

NEAR AND FAR

When you push a car with your hand, you have to touch it. This is a contact force. But some forces can work without touching, too. When your daredevil car is flying through the air, gravity still pulls it down. Gravity is a force at a distance – it can work even across empty space. Weird!

WHAT NEXT?

What happens if you crash marbles into each other? Can you control where they go?

Straw Shooter

Air can push to make things zoom!

YOU WILL NEED

1) An empty squeezy bottle with a narrow spout
2) Straws in two thicknesses – thin ones and slightly wider ones
3) Modelling clay

Here's What to Do...

1. Stick the thinner straw into the opening of the bottle and use modelling clay to seal it in place.

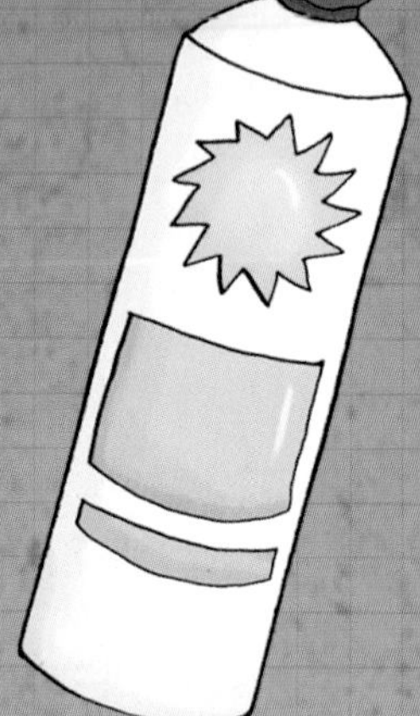

2. Take a wider straw and stick a small lump of modelling clay over the tip to make it airtight.

3. Slide the wider straw over the thinner straw sticking out of the bottle.

4. Pointing the shooter away from people and breakable objects, give it a hard squeeze!

WHAT'S GOING ON?

When you squeeze the bottle, you squeeze the air that's inside it. Some of the air zooms out through the thin straw and pushes against the modelling clay at the end of the wider straw, making it fly away.

TROUBLESHOOTER

There should be no air gaps around the modelling clay – make sure it is sealed tightly.

Air is made of gas, meaning the tiny molecules in it float around freely. You can squeeze them together, but they will bounce back with a pushing force. That's why tyres and inflatables are bouncy. They have squashed or compressed air inside them that pushes outwards.

WHAT NEXT?

Experiment with how far you can shoot the straws.

Make a target to aim at, using a large cardboard box with holes cut in it. Mark each hole with a different score.

Heli~Zoomer

When something pushes in one direction, there is an equal push back the other way. This is one way of making things lift off the ground.

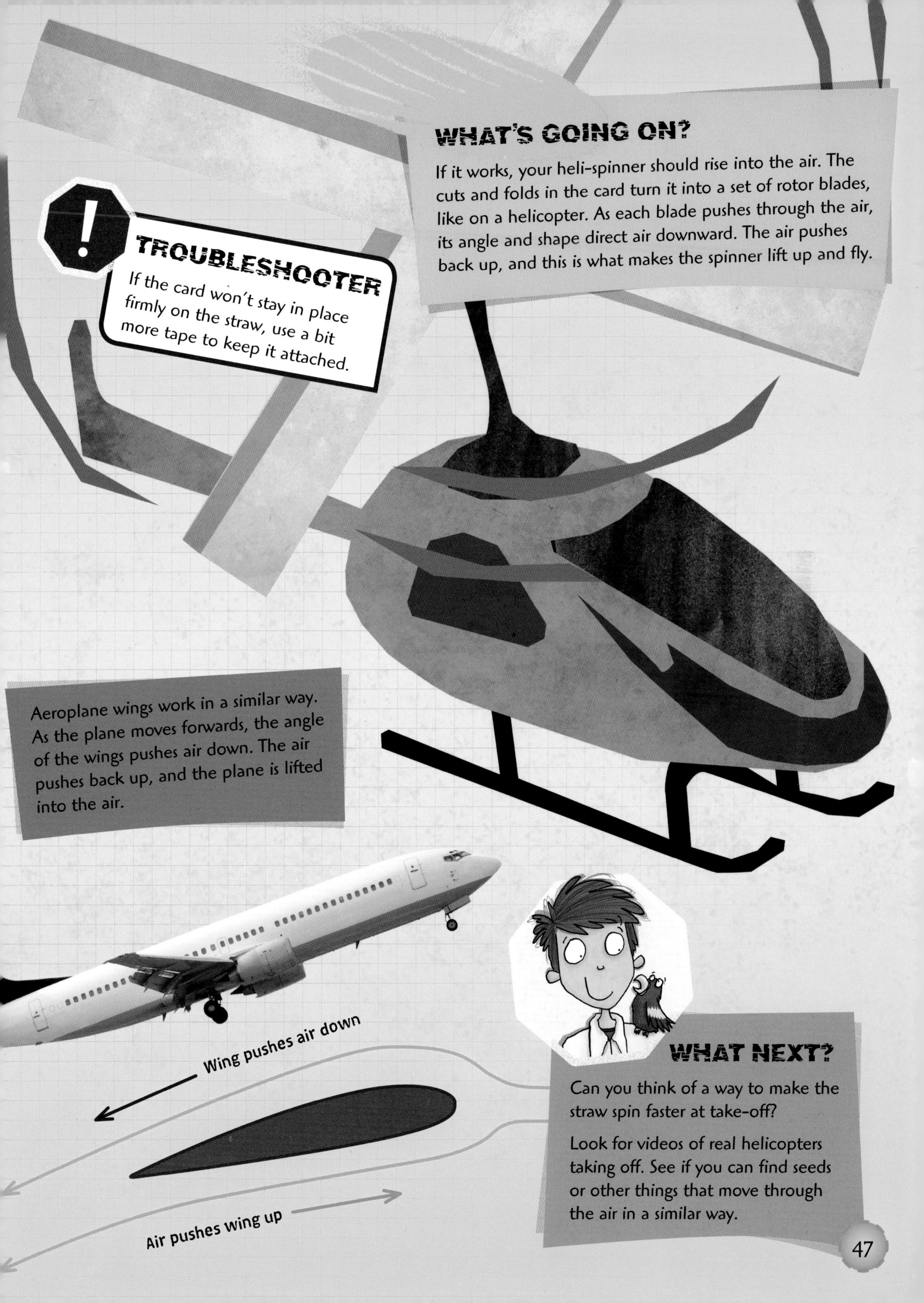

WHAT'S GOING ON?

If it works, your heli-spinner should rise into the air. The cuts and folds in the card turn it into a set of rotor blades, like on a helicopter. As each blade pushes through the air, its angle and shape direct air downward. The air pushes back up, and this is what makes the spinner lift up and fly.

TROUBLESHOOTER

If the card won't stay in place firmly on the straw, use a bit more tape to keep it attached.

Aeroplane wings work in a similar way. As the plane moves forwards, the angle of the wings pushes air down. The air pushes back up, and the plane is lifted into the air.

WHAT NEXT?

Can you think of a way to make the straw spin faster at take-off?

Look for videos of real helicopters taking off. See if you can find seeds or other things that move through the air in a similar way.

Zero-gravity water squirt

What makes water squirt out of a leaky hole? (This experiment is for outdoors!)

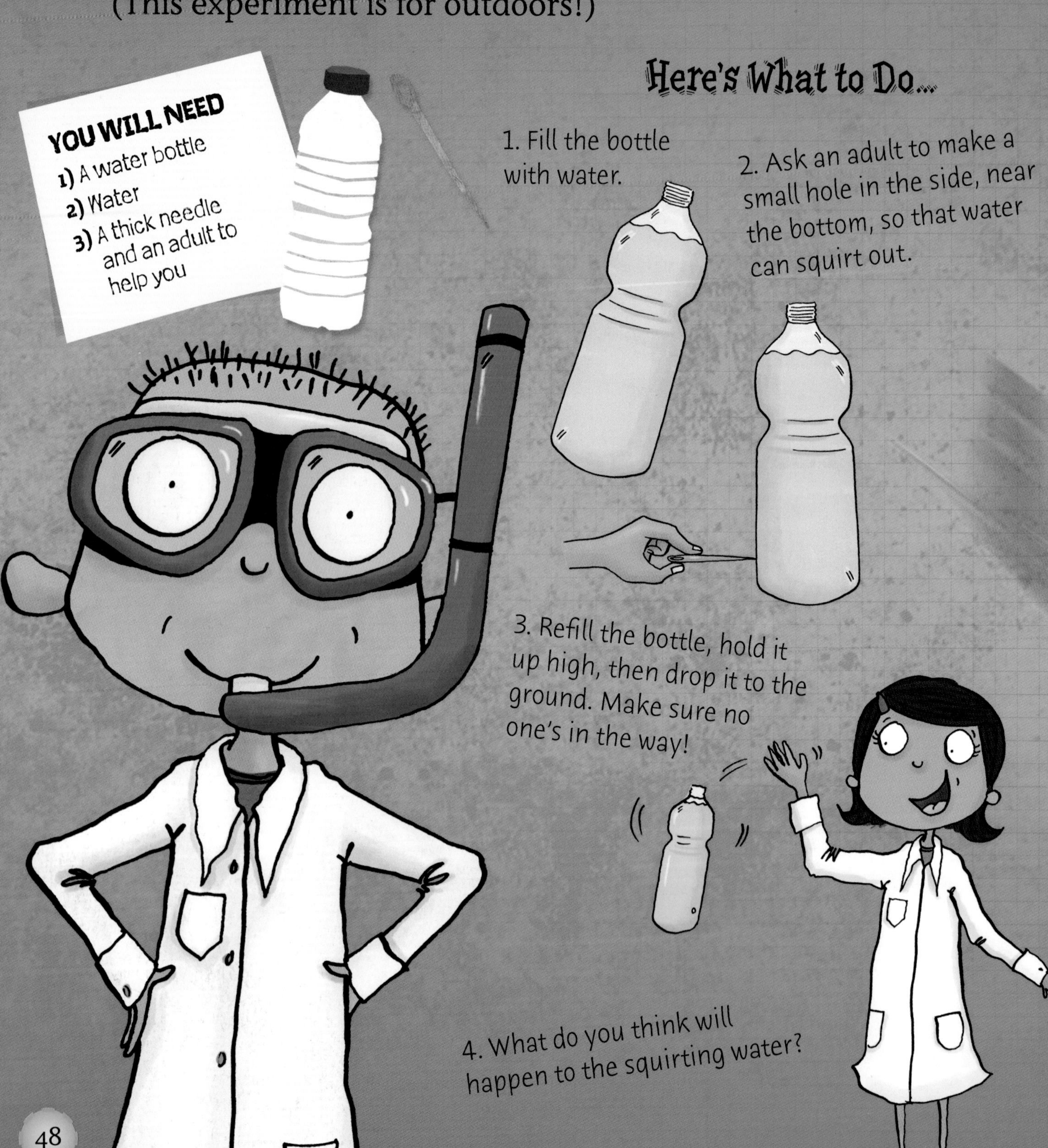

WHAT'S GOING ON?

Gravity pulls down on the water and forces it out through the hole. When you drop the bottle, gravity pulls on the bottle as well as on the water, and they fall at the same speed. That means gravity can't pull the water out. While the bottle is falling, it's as if it is in zero gravity. When it lands, the water will start squirting out again.

SPACE SUCKER

Toilets flush using gravity, but in space that doesn't work, as nothing pulls the water, wee and poo down. Instead, space toilets have to use a sucking force to collect everything.

TROUBLESHOOTER

As the bottle will fall quite fast, you have to watch very carefully to see what happens. If you have a video camera, you could film the experiment and play it back in slow motion.

VOMIT COMET

This plane, called the 'vomit comet' (because it makes you feel sick!), recreates low gravity by zooming downwards. The people inside fall at the same speed, and cannot feel the pull of gravity.

WHAT NEXT?

If you move the bottle upwards quickly instead, would that affect the squirt? Can you think of ways to make the squirt stronger or bigger?

Zooming balloon rocket

You'll be amazed how fast this balloon can zoom!

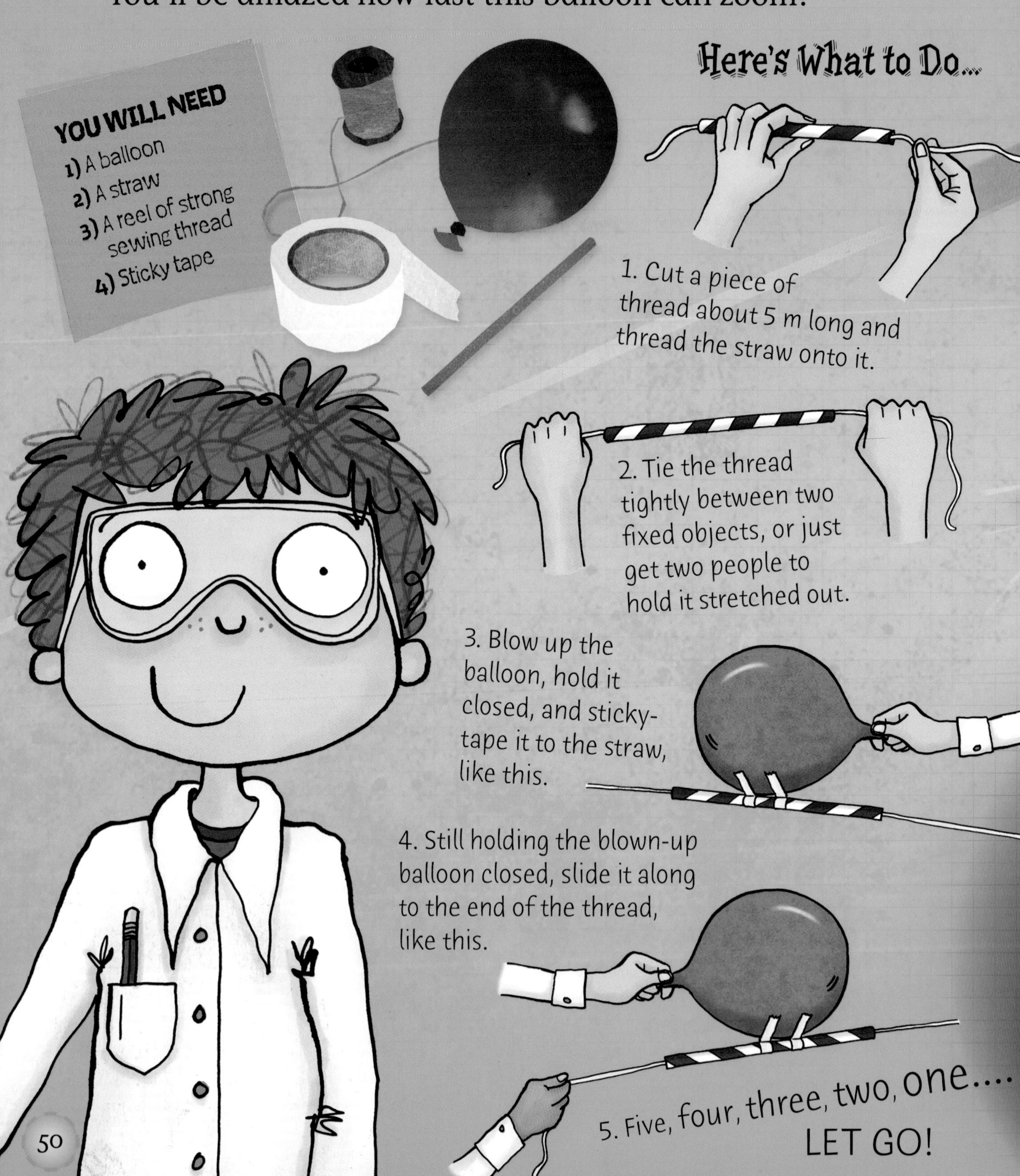

Here's What to Do...

1. Cut a piece of thread about 5 m long and thread the straw onto it.
2. Tie the thread tightly between two fixed objects, or just get two people to hold it stretched out.
3. Blow up the balloon, hold it closed, and sticky-tape it to the straw, like this.
4. Still holding the blown-up balloon closed, slide it along to the end of the thread, like this.
5. Five, four, three, two, one.... LET GO!

WHAT'S GOING ON?

When you let go of the balloon, the air inside comes shooting out, because it's being squeezed hard by the stretchy balloon skin. As the balloon pushes the air out, the air pushes back against the balloon, and the balloon and the straw get pushed forwards.

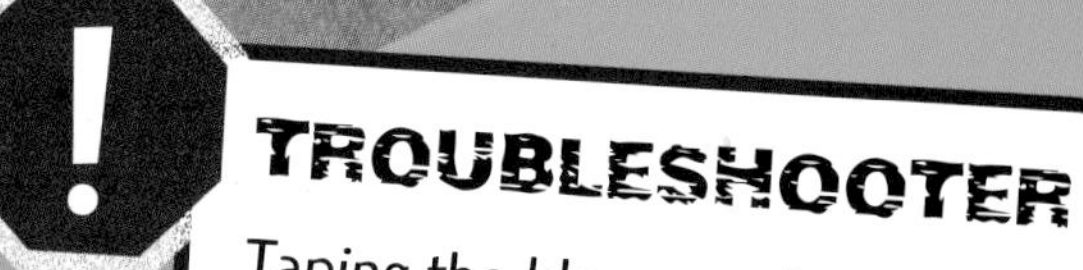

TROUBLESHOOTER

Taping the blown-up balloon to the straw while holding it closed can be tricky – it's easier if two people work together.

FORCES

This experiment shows that whenever there is a pushing force, there is also an equal pushing force in the opposite direction. The balloon pushes out the air – so the air pushes the balloon, making it zoom!

SPACE FORCES

Real rockets in outer space work this way. It doesn't matter that there is no air in space for them to push 'against'. As a rocket blasts out gases in one direction, it gets pushed in the other direction.

WHAT NEXT?

Can you make the balloon zoom upwards like a real rocket taking off? Does it work? When something moves upwards, it has to fight against the pulling force of gravity – so it might not go quite as fast.

Magazine tug-of-war

What mysterious force can stick two magazines together without using any glue?

YOU WILL NEED

Two large magazines, paper pads or books with lots of pages – the thinner the pages, the better

Here's What to Do...

1. Put the two magazines on a table with the edges of the pages facing each other, like this:

2. Now carefully interleave all the pages from both magazines, putting one on top of another in turn, like this:

3. Try pulling the magazines away from each other by their spines. If you can't do it, get two people to try, one pulling each magazine. Take care!

WHAT'S GOING ON?

You would think it would be easy to pull the magazines apart, but it's really hard! This is because of a force called friction. Friction makes surfaces grip onto each other and slow down as they rub past each other. Two sheets of paper rubbing together have some friction, but it's very weak. But when all the pages in the magazines are next to each other, there's so much friction that they grip onto each other very firmly.

TROUBLESHOOTER

It works best if the magazines are roughly the same size.

FRICTION FIRE

Friction also heats objects up as they rub together. That's why rubbing sticks together can make fire! To test this, take two coins and hold them on a pad of paper with your fingertips. Keep one still and rub the other one to and fro very fast for 10 seconds. Does one get hotter?

WHAT NEXT?

Test the friction of different substances by seeing how easily they slide along a table top when pushed. Try a coin, piece of chocolate, a pebble, an eraser, and a plastic or wooden ruler. Which things grip best and which slide most easily?

Jelly slide

Friction is great if you want to get a good grip. But what if you don't? To reduce friction, you can use something slippery, such as oil.

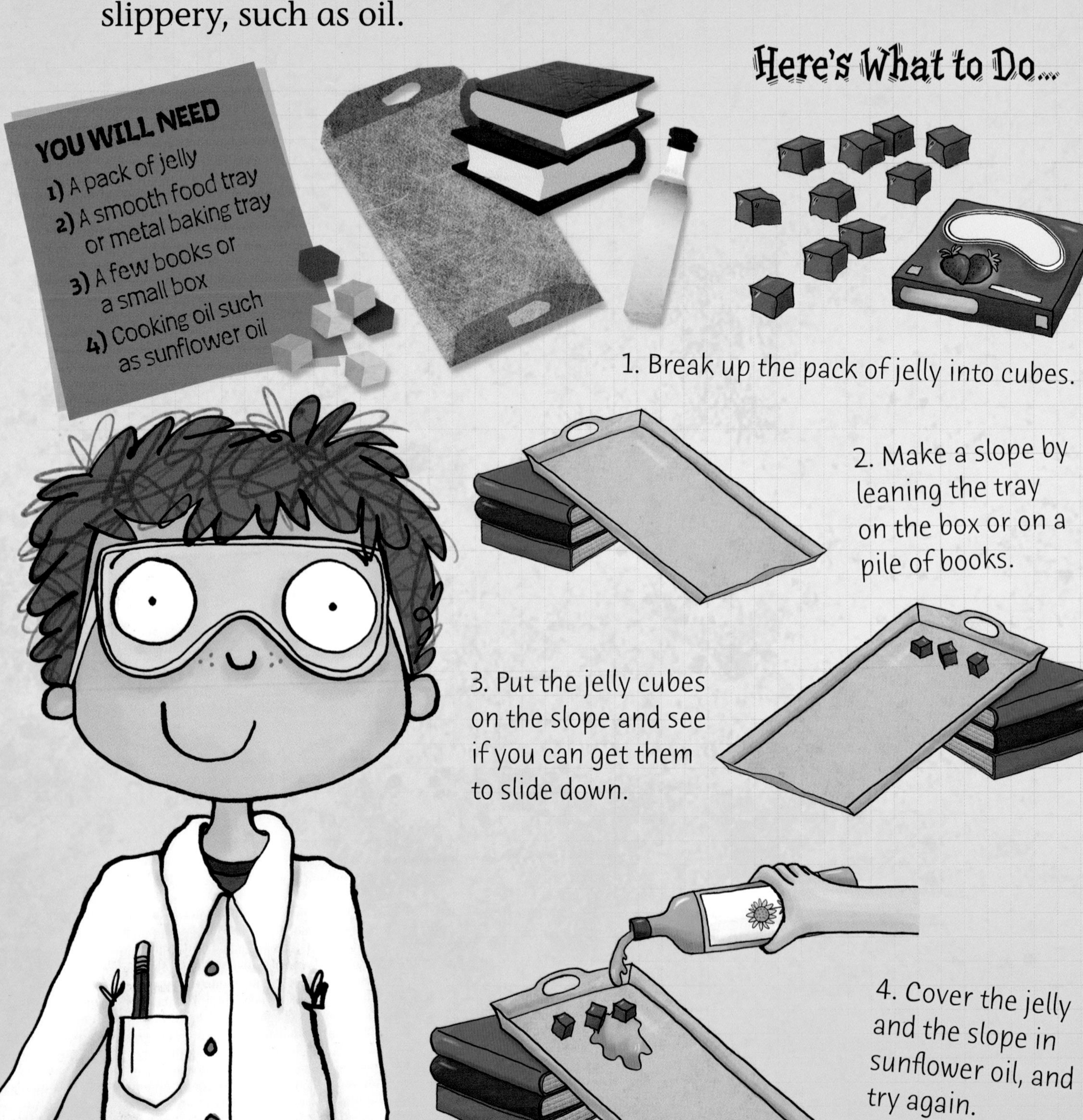

WHAT'S GOING ON?

For friction to work, two surfaces need to rub together. Without oil, tiny bumps and valleys on the surface of the jelly and tray catch and stick to each other. The oil acts as a barrier, separating those surfaces. Other liquids can also reduce friction. For example, it's easier to slip on a wet floor, because the water separates your feet from the floor, making it harder to grip.

TROUBLESHOOTER

If you can't get or don't want to use jelly, cube or rectangle-shaped pencil erasers also work well.

SLIPPERY SKIS

Skiers and snowboarders rub wax on their skis or boards to reduce friction. Wax is thicker than oil and more solid, but still slippery. Because it's thicker, it's better at sticking to and staying on the skis or the board when zooming downhill.

WHAT NEXT?

Set up a jelly-cube downhill race using different liquids, such as cooking oil, water, milk and baby oil. Which reduces friction best?

Flying bucket

When a cup full of water is upside down, the water will fall out. Won't it?

YOU WILL NEED

1) A sturdy paper cup
2) Strong string
3) A large needle
4) Water
5) A safe open space outdoors

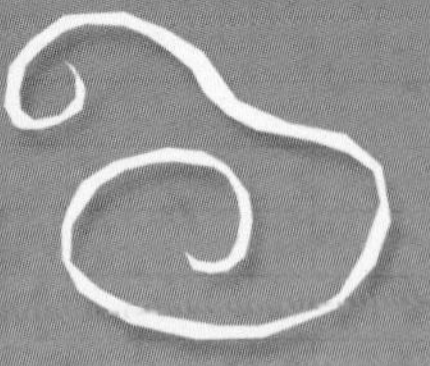

Here's What to Do...

1. Ask an adult to help you make two holes at the sides of the cup, just below the rim.

2. Cut a 1-m long piece of string, put the ends into the holes, and tie them together like this, making a mini-bucket with a long handle.

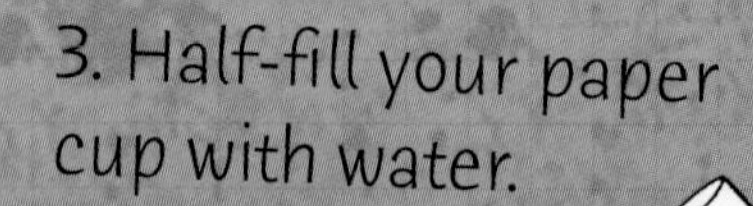

3. Half-fill your paper cup with water.

4. Carefully, outdoors and away from other people, swing the bucket to and fro, then right around in a circle, so it turns completely upside down.

WHAT'S GOING ON?

If you held your cup still and upside down, the force of gravity would pull the water out. But in this experiment, it doesn't!

When objects move, they keep going in the same direction, unless another force makes them change. As the water and cup whirl around, they are trying to keep going in a straight line, pulling away from you. But another force, the pull of the string, stops them from escaping, so they move in a circle instead. The two forces balance each other out, and the water stays in the cup.

TROUBLESHOOTER

To make a stronger bucket, stack two cups together before you start.

PLANETS IN ORBIT

The same force holds the planets in place in our Solar System. They are moving fast and trying to go in a straight line. But the Sun's gravity pulls on them too, making them move in a circle, or orbit, around it. This fairground ride (see right) works in the same way.

WHAT NEXT?

How slowly can you whirl the cup around? Is it possible to let any water escape?

Whirling wind speed meter

Humans have invented all kinds of machines to measure forces. Here's one for measuring the pushing force of the wind.

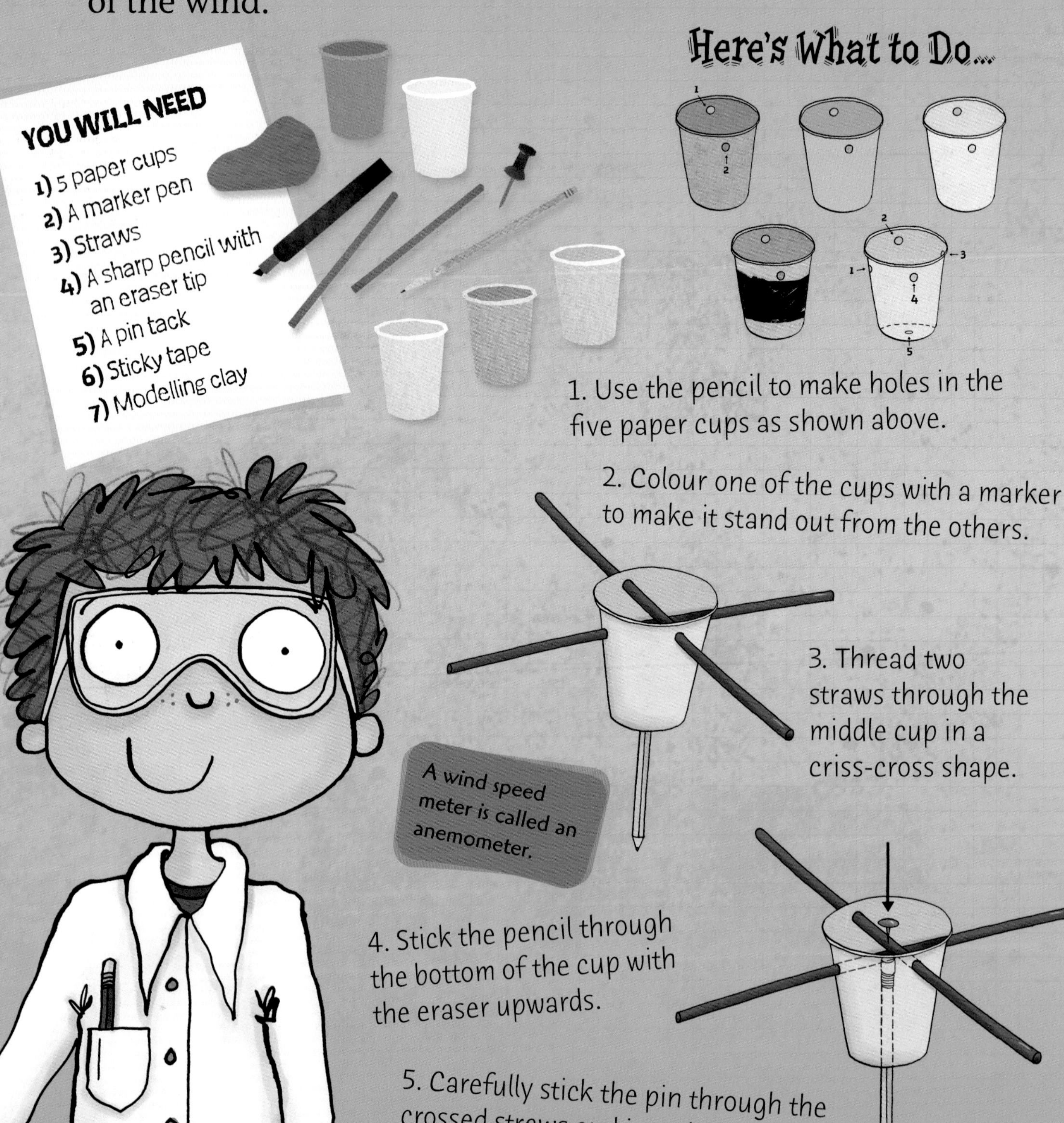

Here's What to Do...

1. Use the pencil to make holes in the five paper cups as shown above.

2. Colour one of the cups with a marker to make it stand out from the others.

3. Thread two straws through the middle cup in a criss-cross shape.

A wind speed meter is called an anemometer.

4. Stick the pencil through the bottom of the cup with the eraser upwards.

5. Carefully stick the pin through the crossed straws and into the pencil eraser, like this:

6. Attach the other four cups to the ends of the straws, like this, and hold in place with tape.

7. Stick the pencil point into a heavy lump of modelling clay, or into the ground.

8. When it's windy, see how fast your anemometer spins round!

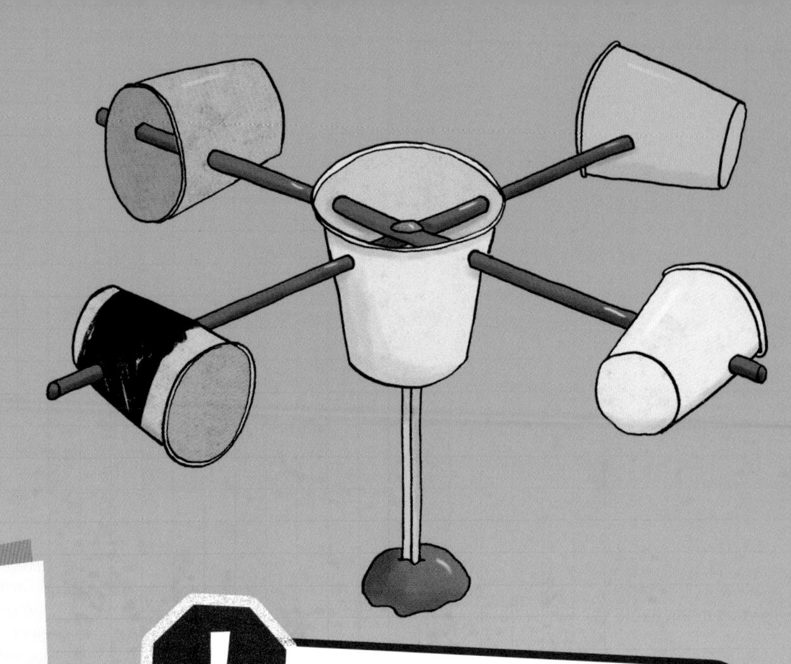

WHAT'S GOING ON?

As the wind blows, it pushes against the anemometer's cups. It flows more easily past the bottom end of each cup, but blows into the open ends, pushing them forward. As they are joined in the middle, they spin around. The faster the wind speed, the faster the anemometer spins.

TROUBLESHOOTER

Don't push the pin down too hard – leave some space for the straws to spin.

Real anemometers at weather stations sometimes work like this too. The fastest wind ever recorded on Earth was a gust of 509 km/h (318 mph) inside a tornado in Oklahoma, USA.

WHAT NEXT?

Measure wind speed by counting how many times the coloured cup goes round in a minute.

Ping pong flinger

Machines use forces to do jobs for us. This ping pong flinger is based on the trebuchet – a weapon invented in medieval times for attacking castles, using the force of gravity.

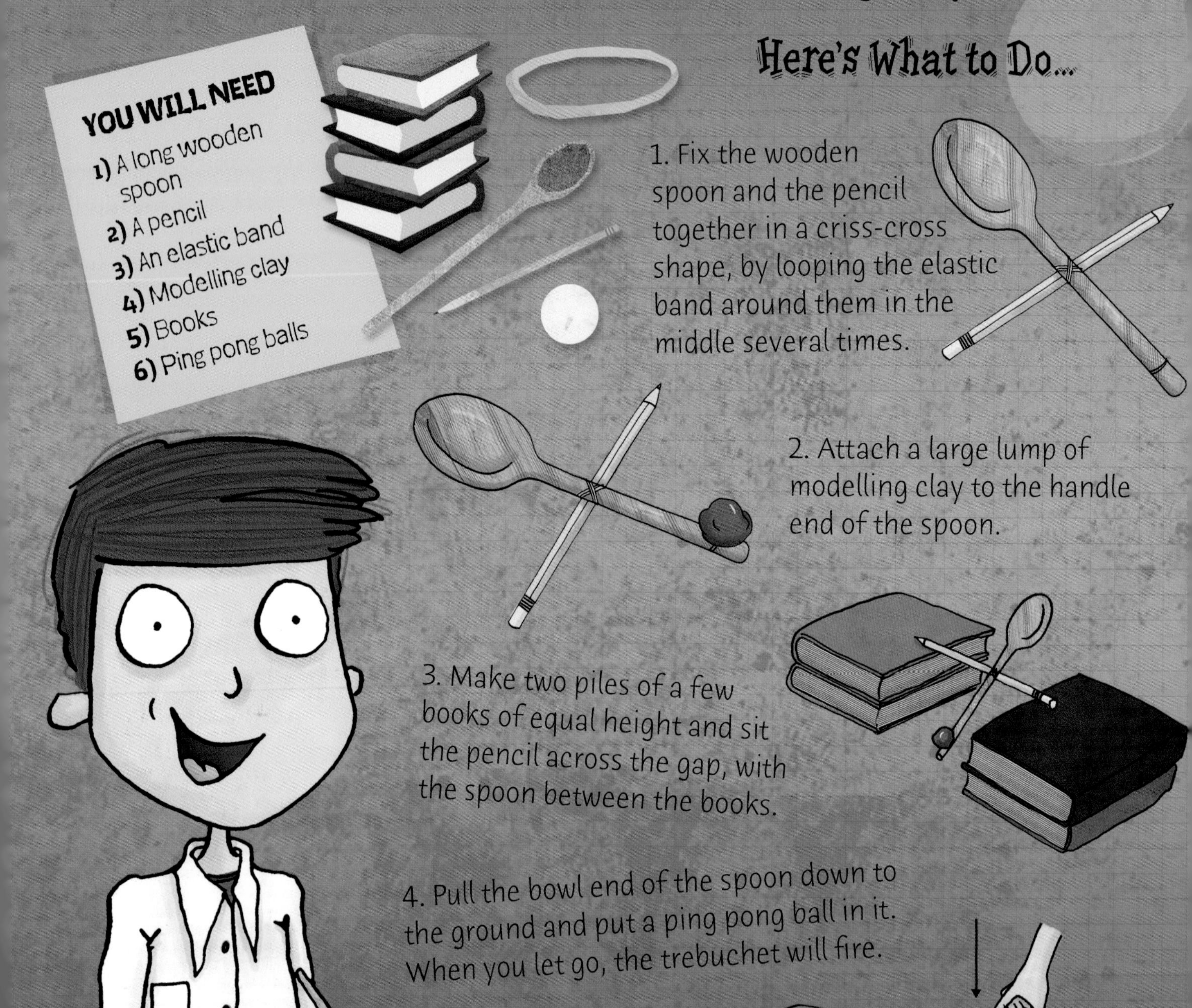

YOU WILL NEED

1) A long wooden spoon
2) A pencil
3) An elastic band
4) Modelling clay
5) Books
6) Ping pong balls

Here's What to Do...

1. Fix the wooden spoon and the pencil together in a criss-cross shape, by looping the elastic band around them in the middle several times.

2. Attach a large lump of modelling clay to the handle end of the spoon.

3. Make two piles of a few books of equal height and sit the pencil across the gap, with the spoon between the books.

4. Pull the bowl end of the spoon down to the ground and put a ping pong ball in it. When you let go, the trebuchet will fire.

WHAT'S GOING ON?

A trebuchet is a type of lever – a long stick or beam with a balancing point, or pivot, in the middle. When you push one end down, the other end goes up, and vice versa. When you let go of the spoon, gravity pulls the heavy end down fast, making the bowl end jerk upwards. It pushes the ping pong ball into the air.

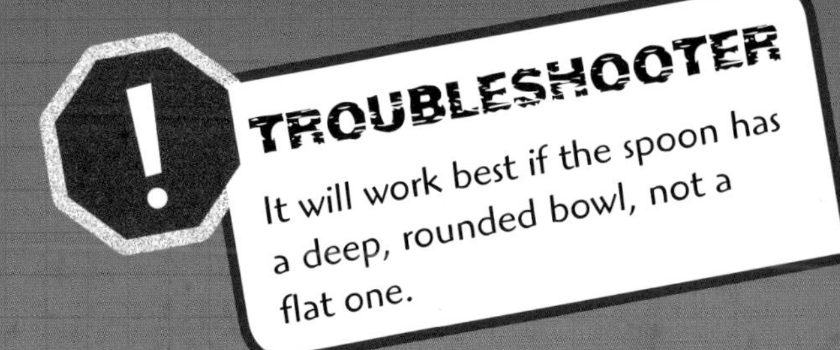

TROUBLESHOOTER

It will work best if the spoon has a deep, rounded bowl, not a flat one.

CASTLE ATTACK!

What did real trebuchets shoot at castles? Not ping pong balls, but heavy rocks, burning torches to start fires, dead animals, and even human heads! Yuck!

WHAT NEXT?

Experiment with different weights, spoons and heights to fire the balls as far or as high as possible. Make a target 'castle' out of a box and see if you can fire the balls inside.

Can you build a more permanent trebuchet model out of lightweight wood or construction toys?

Gas-fuelled rocket

For this rocket, you need a container with a pop-off lid. Wear safety glasses and do this in an open space outside!

YOU WILL NEED

1) A plastic container with a pop-off lid
2) Plain card
3) Sticky tape
4) Felt-tip pens
5) Bicarbonate of soda, also called baking soda
6) A teaspoon
7) Vinegar
8) Tissues

Here's What to Do...

1. Roll a piece of card around your container and tape it in place to make a tube (the lid end of the container should be at the bottom).

2. Decorate your rocket with windows or numbers, and, if you like, a paper nose cone and fins.

3. Put a teaspoon of bicarbonate of soda into a square of tissue and wrap it up.

4. Holding the rocket pointing downwards and the container pointing up, half-fill it with vinegar.

5. Quickly drop in the tissue, press the lid on, turn it over, stand it on the ground and stand well back.

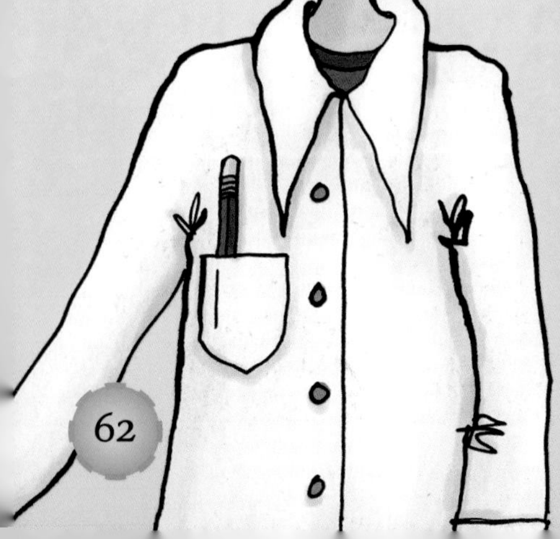

WHAT'S GOING ON?

Whoosh! If it works, your rocket will shoot up into the air as it fills with gas and the lid is forced off. The bicarbonate and vinegar create a chemical reaction that makes carbon dioxide gas. The gas fills up the container until it has such a strong pushing force that it blows the lid off.

TROUBLESHOOTER

If your rocket is too narrow to stand up easily, press it onto a modelling clay base.

WHAT NEXT?

Instead of vinegar, try other weak acids such as lemon juice, orange juice or fizzy water. Which works best?

To see the chemical reaction happen, mix the bicarbonate and acid in a bowl. You'll see the bubbles of gas that provide the pushing force.

Magnet power

Magnets have an amazing pulling and pushing force on each other and on some types of metal. Here are some experiments to try with them.

YOU WILL NEED

1) Magnets of different shapes, sizes and strengths, if possible
2) Everyday metal objects
3) Fine thread
4) Sticky tape

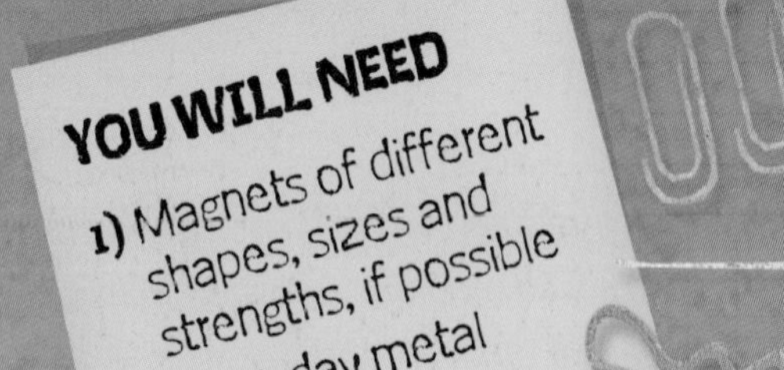

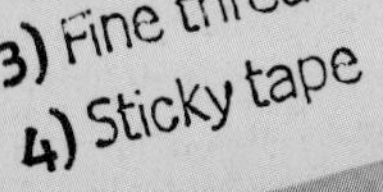

Here's What to Do...

1. Test magnets on different metal objects such as paperclips, pins, coins, hairclips, spoons, pans or your fridge. Which objects do the magnets stick to?

2. Use fine thread to attach metal paperclips to a surface, then use magnets to make them hover in mid-air.

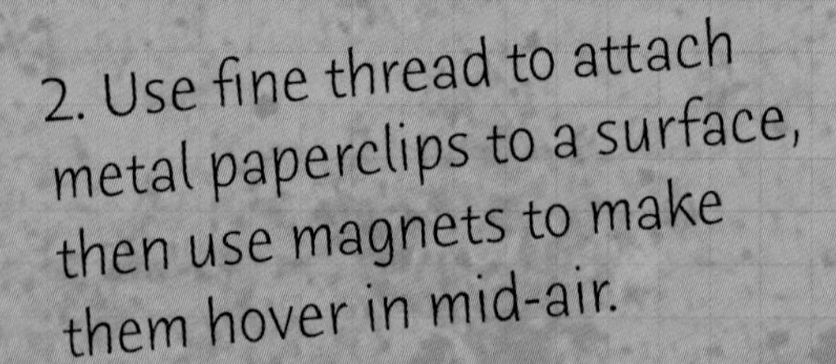

3. Two magnets can push against each other if they are in the right position. Try positioning them so they push apart. Then give two people one of the magnets each and see if they can push them together.

4. Do magnets work through paper, card, wood or your fingers?

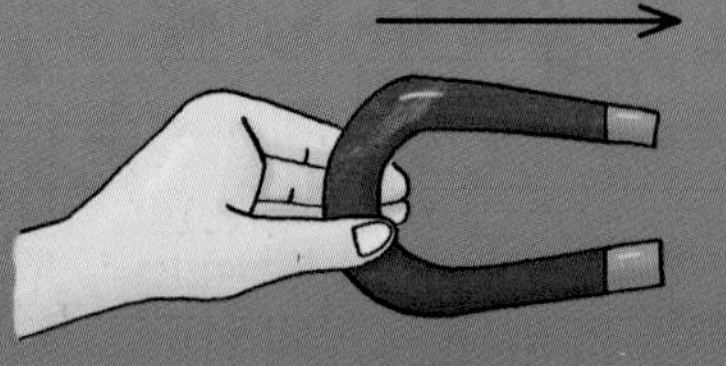

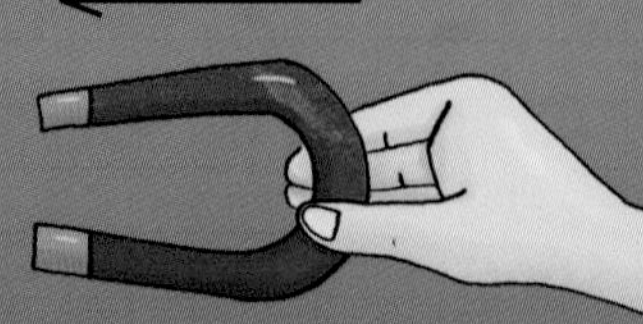

WHAT'S GOING ON?

What is a magnet? It's a piece of metal that creates a magnetic force field around it, which affects some types of metals and other magnets. Magnets can do this because the tiny particles in the metal are arranged in a particular pattern. Only some types of metals can become magnets. They include iron, steel (which contains iron) and nickel.

A magnet's two ends or sides are called its north and south poles. Two different poles will attract each other, while two alike poles will push apart, or repel, each other.

EVERYDAY MAGNETS

We use magnetic force for all kinds of things. Magnets hold up lists on fridges, sort out scrap metals, and make maglev trains (below) float above their tracks. They make credit card readers, speakers, microphones and motors work. The Earth is a giant magnet too, and the magnetic needle in a compass points to its North Pole.

WHAT NEXT?

Can you use magnets to set up a magic trick, making things seem to move by themselves?

Make it Glow!

Glow!

What makes things glow with light? Light is a kind of energy. It travels through the air, spreading out from lamps, streetlights and car headlights. Light also reaches us from much further away – from the Sun and the stars, which shine onto us here on Earth.

LIKE WHAT?

There's light all around us, day and night. Long ago, people only had natural light sources, such as the Sun, Moon, stars, lightning and fires. Today, we can also light up our houses at night using electric lights. Some animals glow with their own light, like fireflies and lantern sharks. Besides light sources, light bounces off other objects to our eyes, which is how we see them.

LIFE WITHOUT LIGHT

What would life be like without the glow of light? Most people are used to depending on light to find their way, read, use a computer, or see each other. If you are completely blind, you can still use your other senses to find out about things. Light is also important for making plants grow.

LOOKING AT LIGHT

We see light because our eyes can detect it. When light enters your eyeballs, they send signals to your brain, so you can understand what you see. You don't think about it much, but your brain is constantly busy, working out what the patterns of light mean.

BEING A SCIENTIST

Use the exciting experiments in this book to try out different ways of making and using glowing light. To do experiments like a real scientist, remember:

1. Follow the instructions and watch what happens carefully.
2. You can record your results by writing down, sketching or taking photos of what happens.
3. Real scientists do experiments a few times over to check they always work.

Light and Shadows

Experiment with making shadows to see how light works.

YOU WILL NEED
1) A hand-held electric torch
2) A pair of hands
3) A selection of objects of different shapes
4) A plain, flat wall

Here's What to Do...

1. Use the torch to shine light at a plain, pale-coloured wall.

2. Try holding an object or your hand up to make a shadow. Twist and turn it to make different shapes.

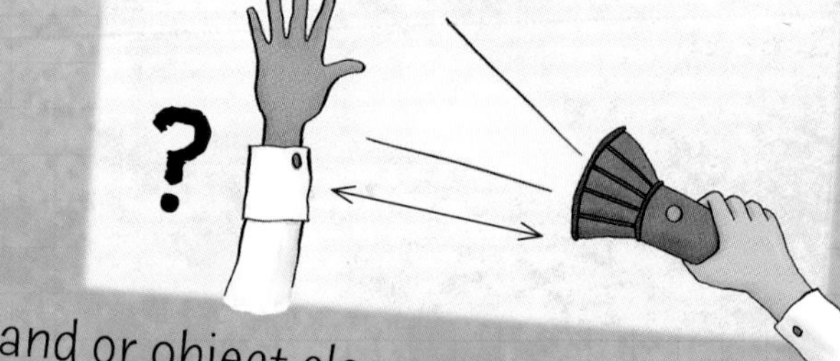

3. Move your hand or object closer to the light, then further away – what happens?

4. Shine your torch through a see-through object, like an ice cube or clear plastic ruler. Does it have a shadow?

WHAT'S GOING ON?

As light shines out from a light source, it travels in straight lines, called beams or rays. If there is something in the way, the light cannot bend around it. Instead, some of the light is blocked, leaving a shadow where the light can't reach. The shadow is the same shape as the object that's in the way.

See-through or transparent objects can have shadows too. This may be because they block a little bit of the light, or because they make the light rays break up and change direction.

TROUBLESHOOTER

Make sure you don't have other lights on in the room.

SHADOW SHAPES

You can use your hands to make shadow shapes that look like animals. Here are some to try:

WHAT NEXT?

Do coloured lights make coloured shadows? To make a coloured light, try putting coloured 3D glasses or sweet wrappers over the end of the torch.

Can you make two shadows at the same time, using two torches?

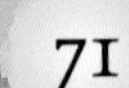

Periscope

Light goes in straight lines, but it can change direction if it bounces off a shiny surface, like a mirror.

YOU WILL NEED

1) A long, narrow cardboard box
2) Scissors
3) Modelling clay
4) Two small mirrors

Here's What to Do...

1. Cut flaps in both ends of your box, as shown.

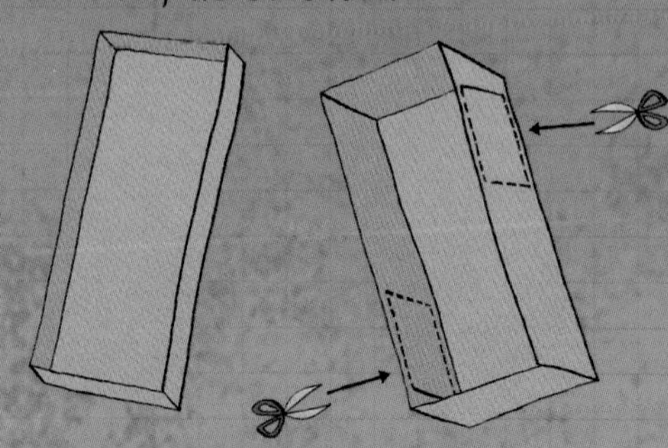

2. Push the flaps into the box to make sloping surfaces each at a 45° angle. Hold the flaps in place by putting lumps of modelling clay behind them.

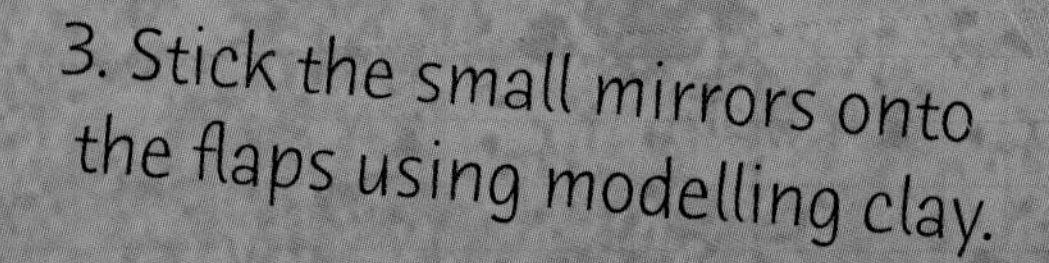

3. Stick the small mirrors onto the flaps using modelling clay.

4. Hold the box upright and look into the bottom mirror. You should be able to see what you would see if you were looking out of the top hole.

WHAT'S GOING ON?

When a beam of light hits a mirror, it reflects, or bounces off it. If it hits the mirror at a right angle, or 90°, it reflects straight back. If it hits at another angle, it reflects off in a different direction. The tilted mirrors in the periscope make the light beams turn round a corner, travel down inside the box, then bend out again to meet your eyes.

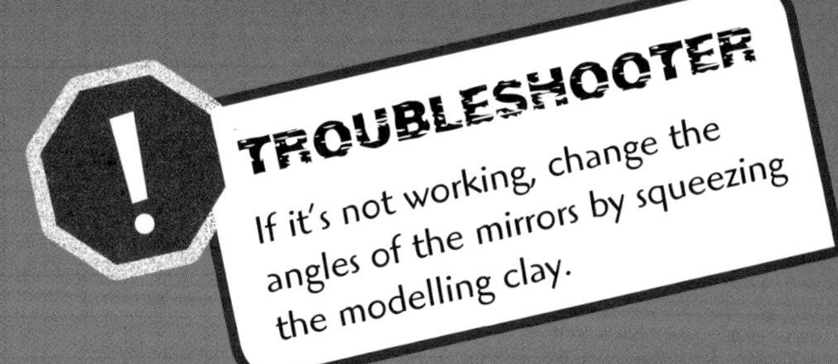

TROUBLESHOOTER

If it's not working, change the angles of the mirrors by squeezing the modelling clay.

Mirror

Light

Mirror

UNDERWATER VIEW

Submarines have periscopes so that the people inside can look out above the surface of the water.

WHAT NEXT?

Try using your periscope to look over a wall or round a corner while you hide behind it.

Can you make light go on an even more complicated journey using more mirrors?

You can decorate your periscope with leaves to camouflage it.

Tea light lanterns

How can you make a tea light candle into a better, brighter light?

YOU WILL NEED

1) 4 tea light candles
2) 4 clear jam jars
3) Thin card
4) Scissors
5) A thick black felt-tip pen
6) Kitchen foil
7) Sticky tape
8) An adult to help – be careful with candles!

Here's What to Do...

1. Cut three rectangles of card. Each one should be as high as your jars and long enough to wrap halfway around them.

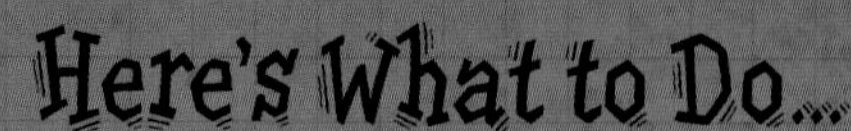

2. Decorate the rectangles as follows:
   - Colour one in all over with the black pen.
   - Cover one with a smooth layer of foil and tape it on at the back.
   - Cover one with foil that has been crumpled up, then opened out again.

3. Now bend the cards around the back of three of the jars, with the decorated surface facing inwards. Tape them in place.

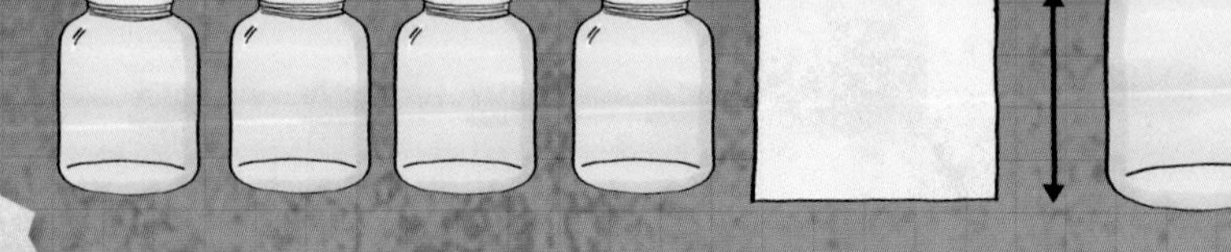

4. Stand the jars in a row on a safe, firm surface, along with the fourth jar with nothing behind it. Put the tea lights in and ask an adult to light them. Stand back, and look at the jars from the front. Which gives the brightest light?

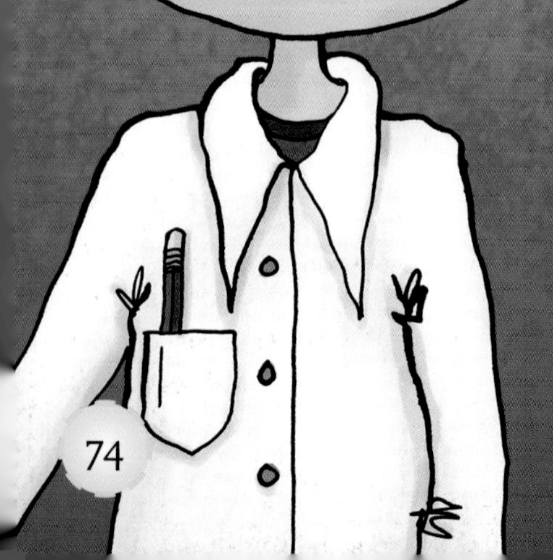

WHAT'S GOING ON?

When a candle glows with light, it shines in all directions. If there is a mirror or shiny surface behind it, the light will bounce back, and more of it will shine at you. The crumpled foil makes light shoot off in all directions, so it doesn't work quite as well. The black surface doesn't reflect much light at all.

TROUBLESHOOTER

It will be easier to see the results if you switch off any other lights in the room.

SHINY LAMPS

Car headlights and torch bulbs have curved mirrors behind them, to help as much light as possible shine forwards.

WHAT NEXT?

What happens if you try other effects, such as covering the card with glitter?

Make an indoor rainbow

This experiment shows how real rainbows are made from light.

YOU WILL NEED

1) A clear glass
2) Water
3) A small mirror that you can get wet
4) A torch
5) White paper or card

Here's What to Do...

1. Fill the glass with water.

2. Stand the mirror in the water, leaning against the side of the glass.

3. Turn the lights off and shine the torch through the water at the mirror.

4. Hold a piece of white paper or card to catch the reflected light. You should see a rainbow pattern!

WHAT'S GOING ON?

This experiment works because of something called refraction – a name for light bending. White light is made of a mixture of all the rainbow colours. When a beam of light moves from one see-through substance into another, it bends slightly. The bending makes the light split into its different colours.

TROUBLESHOOTER

If you don't want to put your mirror in water, you can try holding it behind the glass, and shine the torch at it through the water.

In this experiment, the light shines from air into glass, then into water, then back again. So it bends and splits quite a lot – enough for you to see the colours of the rainbow.

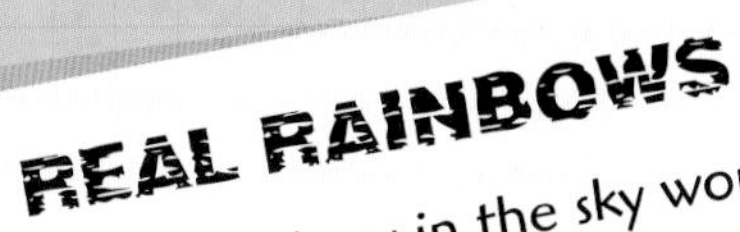

REAL RAINBOWS

A real rainbow in the sky works the same way, but with sunlight and raindrops. Beams of sunlight shine into the raindrops, bounce off the inside and shine back out again, split into rainbow colours.

WHAT NEXT?

Try shining a torch through other clear objects, such as a clear plastic ruler, spectacle lenses, glass ornaments or crystals, to see if they make a rainbow.

Glowing envelopes, plasters and sweets

Explore a very unusual way of making light with these quick experiments.

YOU WILL NEED
1) Sticking plasters
2) Sugar lumps or large-grained sugar
3) A plate
4) A rolling pin
5) Self-seal envelopes
6) Crunchy sweets
7) A mirror

You need somewhere really dark for this, like a room at night, or a dark walk-in cupboard. Take care not to bump into things!

Here's What to Do...

1. Take ordinary sticking plasters – several brands if possible – and try ripping the backing off them as fast as you can.

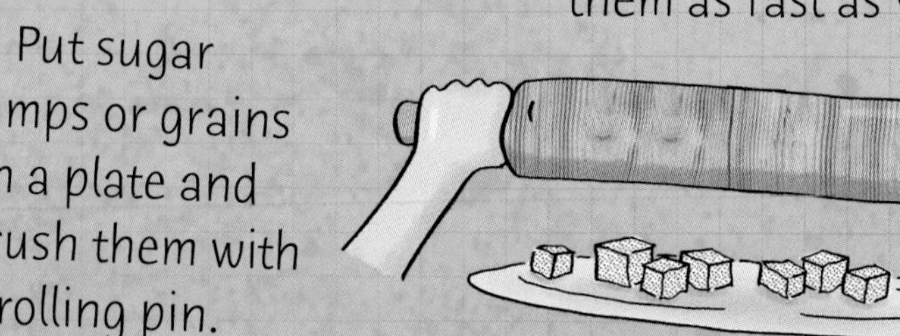

2. Put sugar lumps or grains on a plate and crush them with a rolling pin.

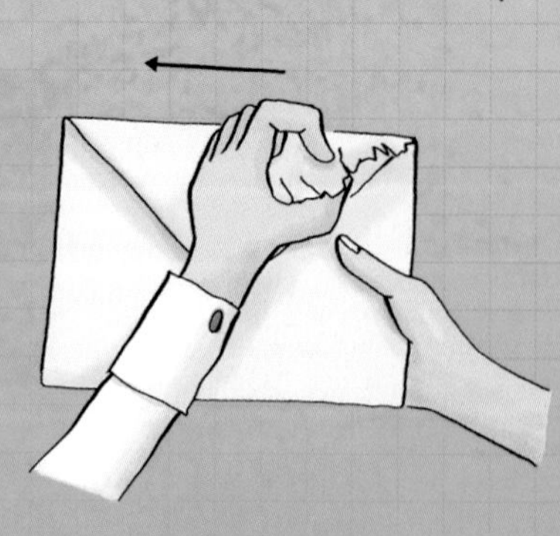

3. Seal up a self-seal envelope, then rip it open again as fast as possible.

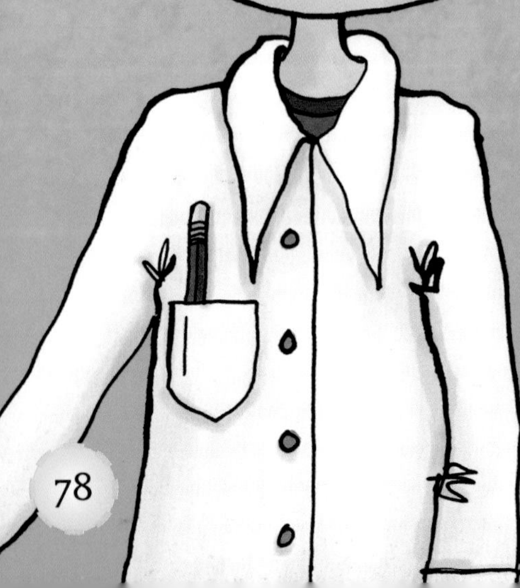

4. Take a hard but breakable sweet, like a hard, crunchy mint, and snap it in two. Or try crunching it with your mouth open in front of a mirror.

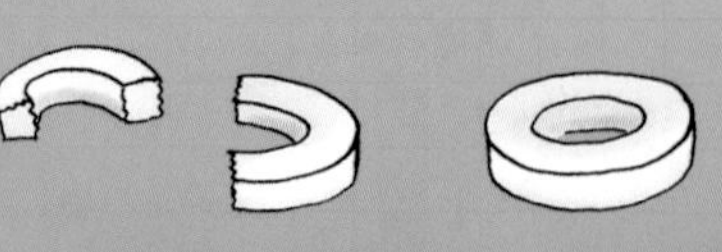

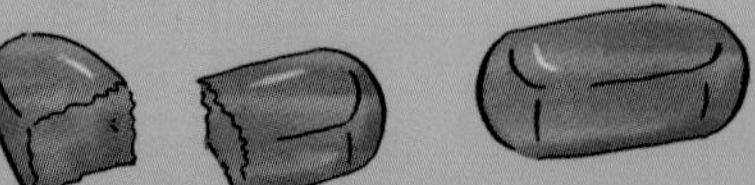

WHAT'S GOING ON?

Amazingly, doing any of these things can create sparks and flashes of bright blueish light, called triboluminescence. It happens because some chemicals spark when their atoms and molecules, the tiny parts they are made of, are pulled apart. Scientists are not sure why!

TROUBLESHOOTER

If you can't see anything, wait a few minutes for your eyes to adjust to the dark.

Long ago, sugar didn't come in grains or lumps. Instead, it was sold in a big, hard cone shape or 'sugar loaf'. People used to notice it sparkling and glowing when they chipped bits off in the dark.

WHAT NEXT?

Can you catch the sparks on camera or video?

Glow-in-the-dark Shapes

Experiment with glow-in-the-dark shapes or stickers, which are easy to find in toy shops.

YOU WILL NEED

1) A packet of glow-in-the-dark stars, moons or other stickers or shapes
2) A bright torch
3) A dark room
4) A book

Here's What to Do...

1. In a dark room, take the stars out of the packet and check they are not yet glowing.

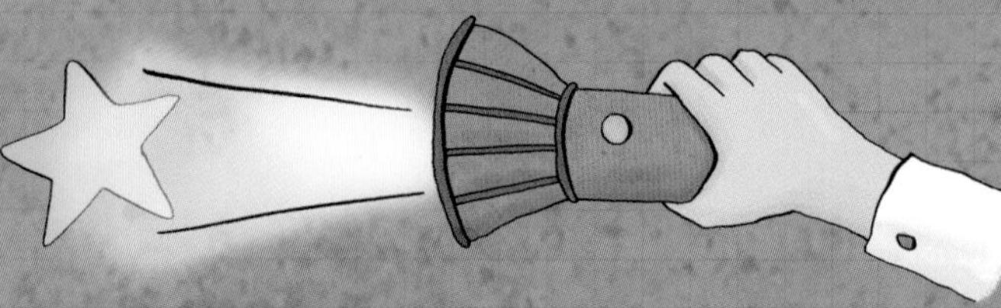

2. Shine a torch on a star for a minute, then switch it off. Does the star glow? How long does it glow for before you can no longer see it?

3. Try leaving a shape or sticker for a day, in sunlight or electric light, half-covered with a book. Does it glow in the dark afterwards?

WHAT'S GOING ON?

Glow-in-the-dark shapes are made of special chemicals that store up energy when light shines on them. Then, they slowly release the energy, making them glow with light. This is called phosphorescence – you say it 'foss-for-RESS-ence'. Only the parts that get 'charged up' with light will glow later.

TROUBLESHOOTER

You need to use shapes that aren't already glowing – if they are, keep them somewhere dark for a few hours first.

GLOWING LIFE

The word 'phosphorescent' is also sometimes used to describe living things that glow in the dark, like some mushrooms, jellyfish and plankton – though they don't work the same way.

WHAT NEXT?

How could you use glow-in-the-dark stars to leave someone a secret message? You would need to make part of each star light up to show a letter or symbol.

Make a glowing jar lantern

You can also buy glow-in-the-dark paint, which lets you make your own glowing creations!

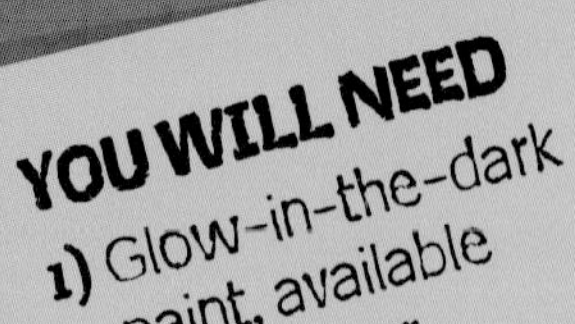

YOU WILL NEED

1) Glow-in-the-dark paint, available from toy or craft shops
2) An empty, clear glass food jar
3) An old newspaper
4) A fine paintbrush

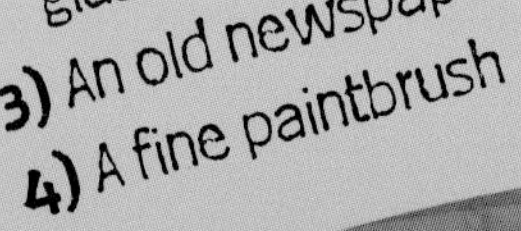

Here's What to Do...

1. Make sure your jar is clean and completely dry. Stand it on an old newspaper.

2. Squeeze a blob of glow-in-the-dark paint onto the newspaper.

3. Use the paintbrush to paint different sizes of dots all over the inside of the jar.

You can buy glow-in-the-dark paint in different colours, to make multicoloured lanterns.

4. Let the paint dry and stand the jar in daylight for a day so the paint can store up light energy. Then you can use it as a decoration or night light when it's dark.

WHAT'S GOING ON?

Inventors have worked out how to make glow-in-the-dark chemicals into safe, non-toxic paint for craft projects. Once it dries, it works just like a glow-in-the-dark shape or sticker.

TROUBLESHOOTER

Work from the bottom of the jar upwards, so you don't smudge the dots you've already done.

USEFUL GLOW

As well as being fun, glow-in-the-dark paint is used on things like clocks, dials and safety signs so that people can see them in the dark.

WHAT NEXT?

People often make lots of these jars to hang up as garden lights, or to use as decorations for parties or weddings.

Glow stick photos

Glow sticks are little sticks that glow when you snap and bend them. You can use them to make a shape picture in the dark. You'll need an assistant to take the photo.

YOU WILL NEED

1) One or more glow sticks
2) A camera or cameraphone
3) A dark room

Here's What to Do...

1. Set up the camera ready to take a picture in low light, with no flash, and a long shutter speed. Ask an adult to help you set a long shutter speed of 20-30 seconds. You may be able to do this with a smartphone app, too.

2. Go into a dark room with the camera, glow stick and photographer!

3. Stand in front of the camera and break your glow stick to make it light up.

4. Wave the glow stick around quickly in a simple shape or pattern. It could be an initial, a love heart, a circle, a wiggly snake or just a squiggle. The other person should take a photo while the stick is moving.

WHAT'S GOING ON?

As long as the camera is on a low light setting with no flash it should be able to capture the fast-moving glow stick as a line or pattern on the photo. When a camera takes a picture slowly like this, there is time for light to move and change in the same photo.

TROUBLESHOOTER

The camera should be held as still as possible. Rest it on a piece of furniture, or use a tripod if you have one.

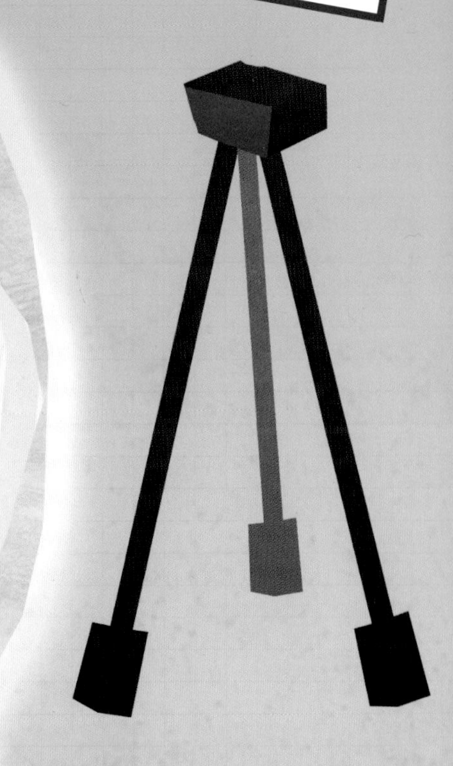

WHAT NEXT?

Try looking at a glow stick or lamp in the dark for a few seconds, then shut your eyes. You should still be able to see the shape of the stick! When bright light hits the light-sensing retina at the back of your eye, it makes it less sensitive. Afterwards, you can still see the shape where the retina is not working as well.

Glowing water stream

This experiment lets you make light curve along a stream of water. It works best in a fairly dark room. (Don't switch the lights off until the experiment is set up!)

WHAT'S GOING ON?

As the light beam moves along inside the water, it actually reflects off the inside surface of the water stream. It bounces to and fro, meaning it can travel wherever the water stream takes it.

TROUBLESHOOTER

It could be messy! Put an old towel or newspaper on the floor to catch drips.

OPTICAL FIBRES

Your water stream is just like a real optical fibre, a bendy tube made of glass for carrying light. Optical fibres can be used to make lamps, or to light up the insides of people's bodies so doctors can look for problems. We also use them to carry computer signals, in the form of on-and-off patterns of light.

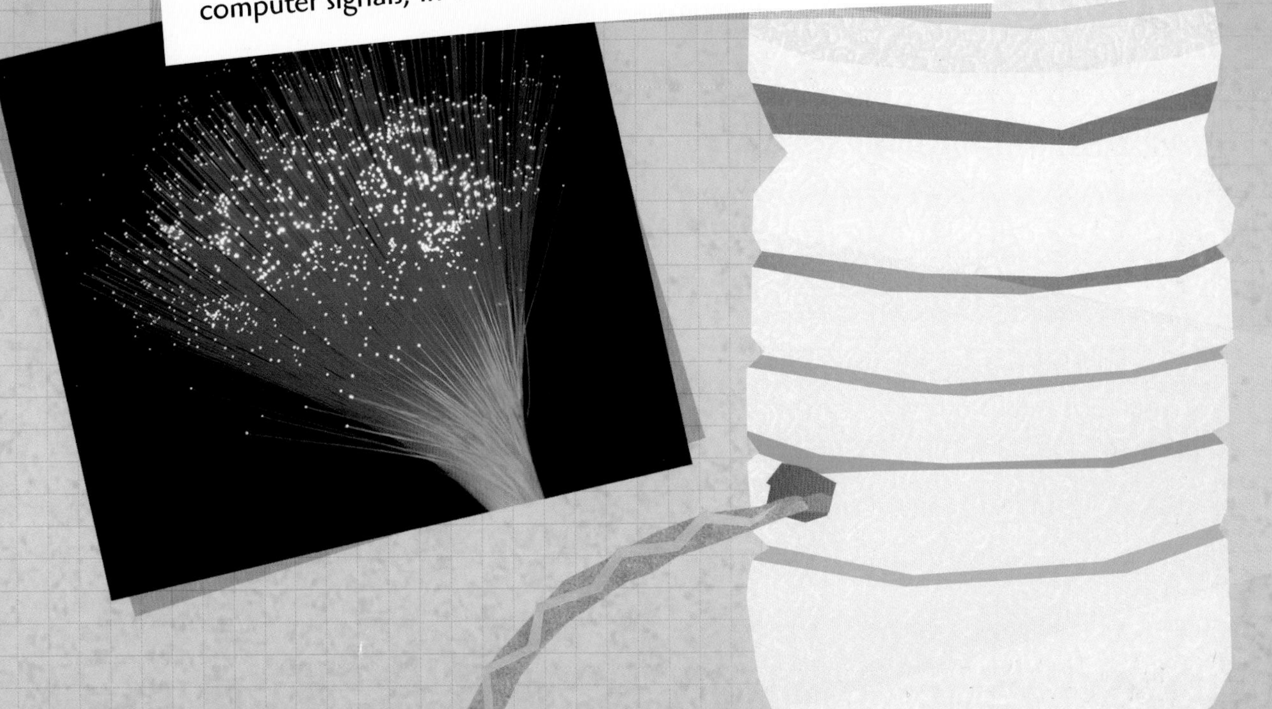

WHAT NEXT?

If you have a laser pointer, try using that instead of a torch – it may work even better.

Laser jelly

Jelly experiments are a great way to find out how light can bounce, bend and travel in different directions. For this you need a laser pointer.

YOU WILL NEED

1) A packet of red or yellow jelly
2) A shallow tray or baking tray
3) Cooking oil
4) A non-sharp knife and pastry cutters
5) A laser pointer

Be careful with laser pointers and don't shine them at your eyes.

Here's What to Do...

1. Make up the jelly using a little less water than usual. Grease the tray with a little oil and pour in the jelly to set.

2. When it's set, cut the jelly into shapes such as strips, D-shapes, squares, triangles and circles, using smooth pastry cutters or a knife.

3. Carefully lift out the shapes and lie them on a flat table top.

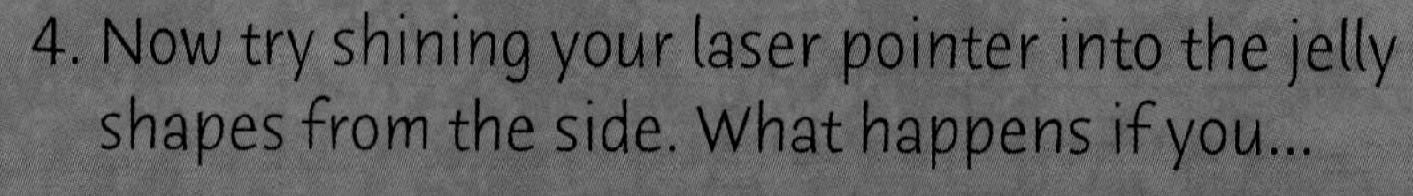

4. Now try shining your laser pointer into the jelly shapes from the side. What happens if you...

- Shine it into the flat side of a D-shape?
- Shine it along inside a jelly strip and wave it from side to side?
- Shine it through a square or triangle?

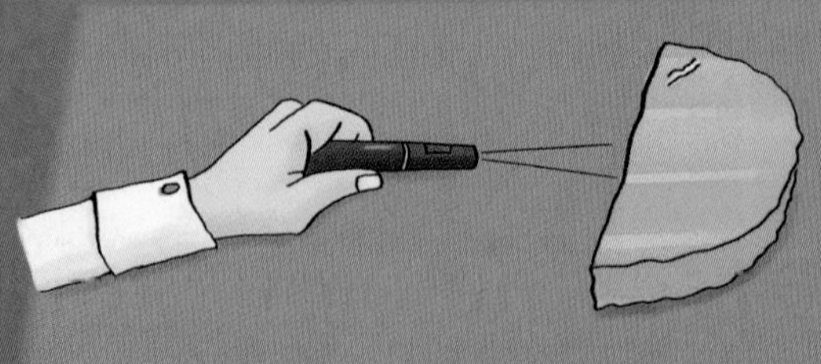

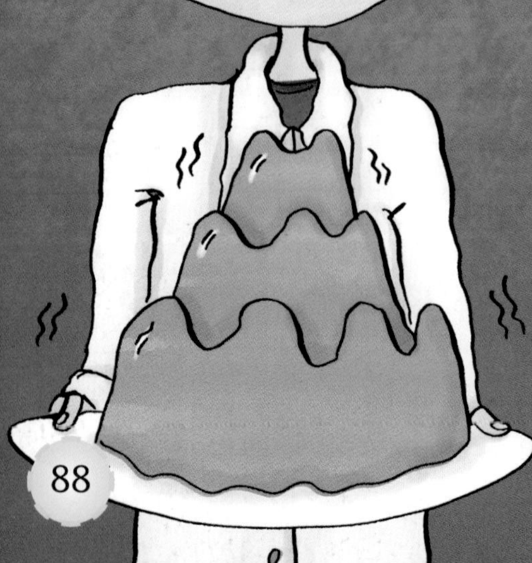

WHAT'S GOING ON?

Depending on the shapes you use, and the angles you point at, different things will happen to your beam of laser light. It may reflect off the inside of a jelly shape, and bounce back out. Or it may shine through a shape, but bend because of refraction.

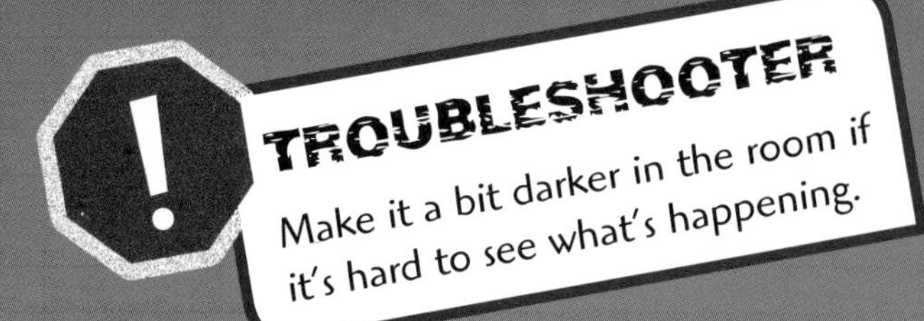

TROUBLESHOOTER

Make it a bit darker in the room if it's hard to see what's happening.

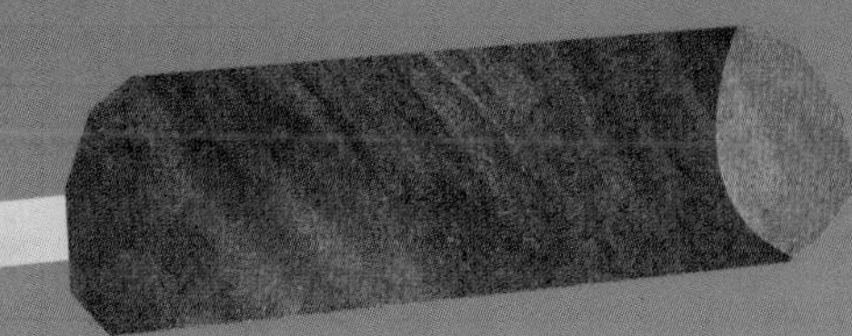

WHAT NEXT?

Try other colours of jelly. Do they work as well?

Can you make a flexible jelly strip into an optical fibre by bending it?

Camera obscura

The first ever type of camera, invented around 1000 years ago, captures a moving picture made of light! You need a room that you can make very dark even when it's bright and sunny outside.

YOU WILL NEED

1) A room with a small window facing a plain, white or light coloured wall
2) A large piece of cardboard or thick black cloth
3) Strong masking or packing tape
4) Pointy scissors or a sharp pencil

Here's What to Do...

1. Cover the window completely with the cloth or cardboard and fix it with masking tape around the sides so no light can get in.

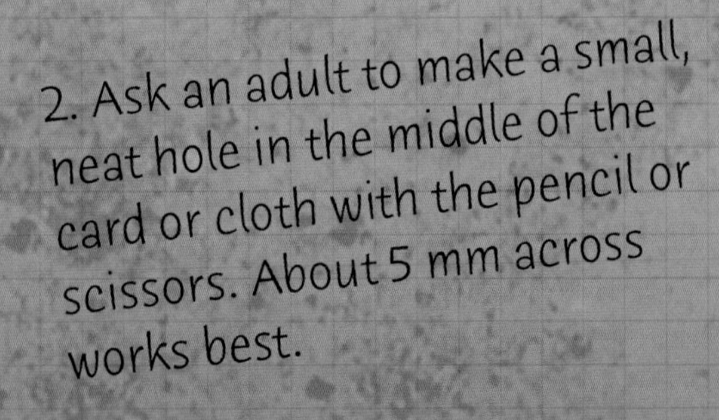

2. Ask an adult to make a small, neat hole in the middle of the card or cloth with the pencil or scissors. About 5 mm across works best.

3. Turn off the light in the room (take care). You should now be able to see a detailed image of what's outside on the wall opposite the window.

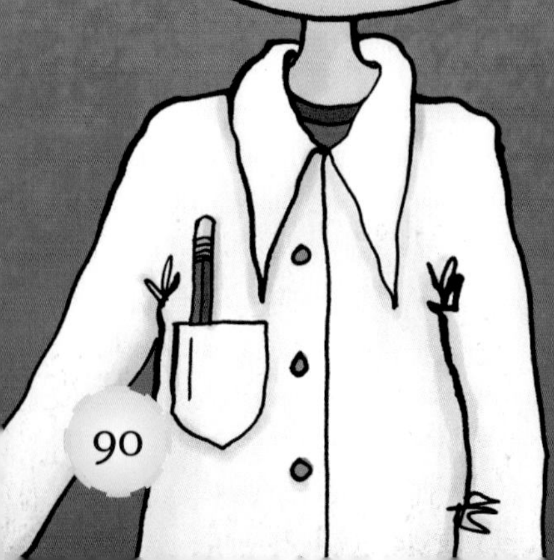

4. Look out for people, trees, clouds or cars moving! What do you notice about the image?

WHAT'S GOING ON?

This type of camera is called a camera obscura, which simply means 'dark room'. The small hole lets in beams of light from the objects outside. As they travel in straight lines, beams from high up end up low down on the wall, and vice versa, so the image is upside down.

TROUBLESHOOTER

Once the room is dark, it will be easy to spot any gaps around your blind and seal them up with tape.

LIGHT SCIENTIST

A scientist known as Alhazen, living in Egypt around the year 1020, studied the camera obscura and figured out how it worked. He also realised that our eyeballs work in the same way.

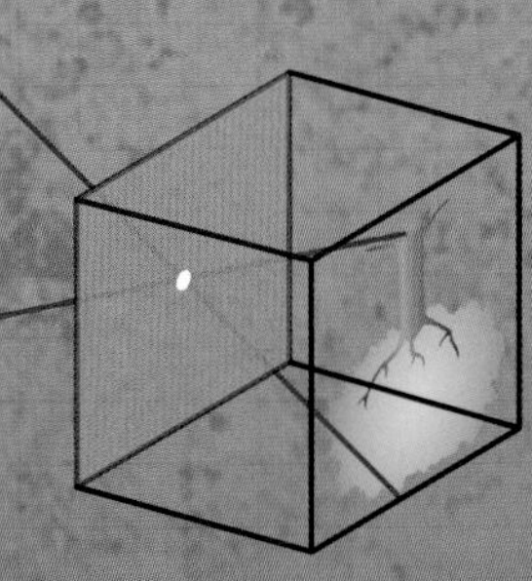

Big camera obscuras like this one in Edinburgh, UK, capture images of the whole city around them.

WHAT NEXT?

Can you make a smaller camera obscura inside a box?

Ultraviolet glow

An ultraviolet (UV) lamp or 'blacklight' shines ultraviolet light. This is a type of high-energy light that is invisible to humans. However, it makes some substances, such as tonic water, glow with light that you can see.

YOU WILL NEED

1) A blacklight or UV torch
2) A bottle of tonic water
3) Laundry liquid
4) Bright white paper
5) Whitening toothpaste
6) Petroleum jelly
7) Overripe bananas

Here's What to Do...

1. Shine your blacklight at the bottle of tonic water in the dark. You will see it glowing bright blue all the way through.

2. Test other substances to see if they glow in a blacklight. You may have some luck with bright white paper, laundry liquid (don't let it touch your skin), whitening toothpaste, petroleum jelly, or even the black spots on ripe bananas.

3. Make secret messages that can only be seen using a blacklight, by writing with a brush and laundry liquid, then leaving it to dry.

WHAT'S GOING ON?

Some substances naturally glow in UV light, such as quinine, found in tonic water. Normal sunlight contains some UV light. So by adding these substances to things like laundry liquid and toothpaste, we can make things like teeth and white clothes appear extra bright and glowing.

You can find small UV torches and lamps at hardware shops. An adult should help you with this.

Scorpions also glow in UV light!

WHAT NEXT?

Freeze tonic water inside a clean rubber glove to make an ice hand that you can stand in a bowl of punch for a spooky party. Use your blacklight to light it up!

Make it
change!

Change!

Change is happening all the time, all around us. Leaves turn brown in the autumn, puddles dry up and disappear in the sun, and clouds turn into rain, which falls on your head. You boil an egg, and it turns hard. You heat some butter, and it melts! Old cars get covered in rust, and old people's hair turns white. But why do things change?

LIKE WHAT?

All the things around us are made of tiny parts called atoms, and molecules – which are made of atoms joined together. When things warm up, cool down, or are mixed together, this can make the atoms and molecules behave differently.

MMM, SMELLS FRESH!

Washing is wet when you hang it up, then it changes and becomes dry in the breeze and sunshine.

TURN UP THE HEAT

Heating things up makes atoms and molecules move faster and separate from each other, which can make a solid like chocolate melt into a liquid.

MAKING MIXTURES

When some substances are mixed together, it causes a chemical reaction, which can make one substance change into another.

YUM, YUM!

BEING A SCIENTIST

In this book there are lots of easy experiments that let you explore amazing, surprising and exciting changes. But don't forget to keep your scientist's hat on!

1. Follow the instructions and watch what happens carefully.
2. Do experiments more than once if you can, to check they always work the same way.
3. Keep a record of your results by writing them down, drawing pictures or taking photos of them.

Turn a penny green

Copper coins normally look a dull brown colour. Try making them change colour using a chemical reaction.

YOU WILL NEED

1) A small mixing bowl
2) A cup for measuring
3) Water
4) White vinegar
5) Table salt
6) A teaspoon
7) Old, well-used copper coins
8) Kitchen paper

Here's What to Do...

1. Half-fill the bowl with water and stir in half a cup of white vinegar and a teaspoon of salt.

2. Take a copper coin and hold it halfway into the water for 20 seconds. What happens?

3. Now drop some more coins into the water and leave them there for 5 minutes.

4. Carefully take them out and lay them on some kitchen paper for an hour. What happens?

WHAT'S GOING ON?

Coins become dull because they react with the air and get a coating on them. When you dip a coin into your mixture, the acid in the vinegar dissolves the coating, making the coins shiny.

However, if you leave the coins covered with the salt and acid, it helps them to react more quickly with the air, creating a green coating (called malachite) that's made of copper and oxygen, a gas found in the air.

The Statue of Liberty is made of copper and was shiny brown to start with. She has now turned green due to chemical reactions.

TROUBLESHOOTER

Don't dry or wipe the coins when you take them out – leave them wet on top.

WHAT IS A CHEMICAL REACTION?

A chemical reaction happens when substances mix together. But not all mixtures cause a reaction. It only happens if the molecules can easily rearrange themselves to make new molecules.

WHAT NEXT?

Vinegar is a type of chemical called an acid. Some other household substances are acids too, like lemon juice and fizzy drinks (cola or lemonade). See if the experiment works if you use them instead of vinegar.

Lava volcano

Use this exciting chemical reaction to make a model volcano erupt.

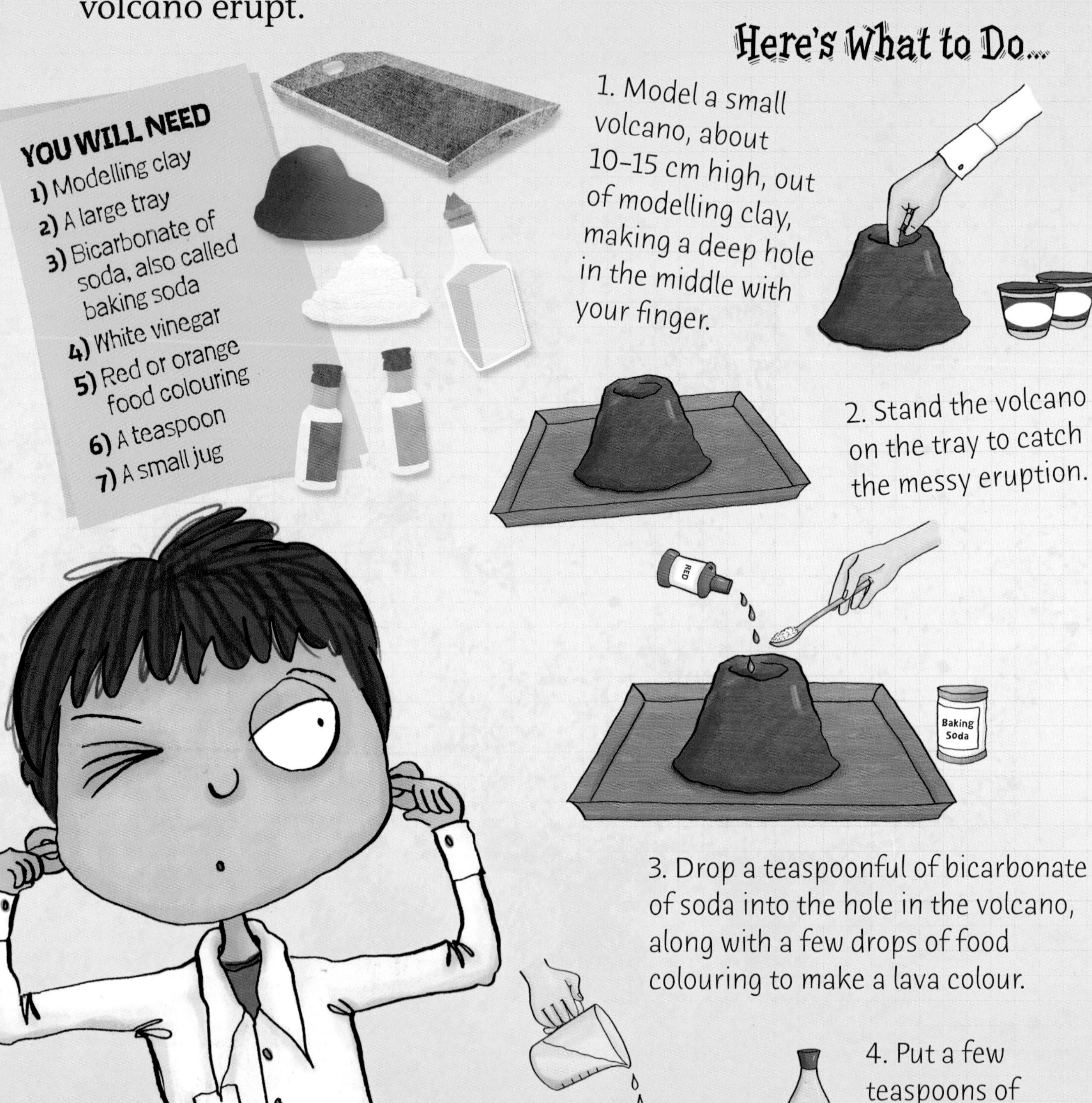

YOU WILL NEED

1) Modelling clay
2) A large tray
3) Bicarbonate of soda, also called baking soda
4) White vinegar
5) Red or orange food colouring
6) A teaspoon
7) A small jug

Here's What to Do...

1. Model a small volcano, about 10–15 cm high, out of modelling clay, making a deep hole in the middle with your finger.

2. Stand the volcano on the tray to catch the messy eruption.

3. Drop a teaspoonful of bicarbonate of soda into the hole in the volcano, along with a few drops of food colouring to make a lava colour.

4. Put a few teaspoons of white vinegar into the jug, then pour it carefully into the hole.

WHAT'S GOING ON?

When the acid vinegar meets the bicarbonate of soda, there's a strong, sudden chemical reaction. The ingredients change, making different, new substances instead. One of these is a gas called carbon dioxide. The bubbles of gas turn the mixture into a frothy foam that expands (gets bigger) and bursts out of the volcano like lava.

TROUBLESHOOTER

Make sure the hole isn't too filled up with the bicarbonate of soda – leave plenty of space for vinegar.

TASTY BUBBLES

Carbon dioxide is often found in food – it's what makes the bubbles in bread and fizzy drinks.

WHAT NEXT?

Try mixing a little bicarbonate of soda and vinegar inside a sealable food bag, then quickly seal it shut. Do this outside and stand well back! The expanding gas will pop the bag open.

The red cabbage test

Use red cabbage to create colour-changing chemical reactions.

YOU WILL NEED

1) A fresh red cabbage
2) A grater
3) A mixing bowl
4) Water
5) A rolling pin
6) A sieve
7) 6 paper or plastic cups

Here's What to Do...

1. Grate a few tablespoons of red cabbage into the bowl and add enough water to cover it.

2. Mash or crush the cabbage with the rolling pin until the water turns purple.

3. Sieve the mixture to get out the cabbage lumps, and keep the liquid.

4. Pour a little of the liquid into each of your cups.

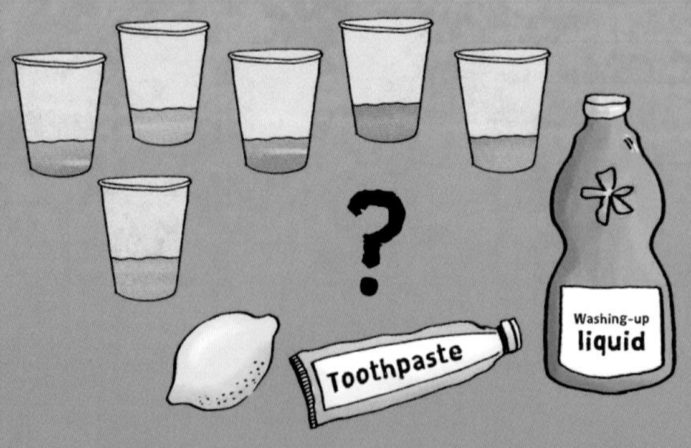

5. Now test different substances by dropping a little of them into a cup, and looking at what happens.

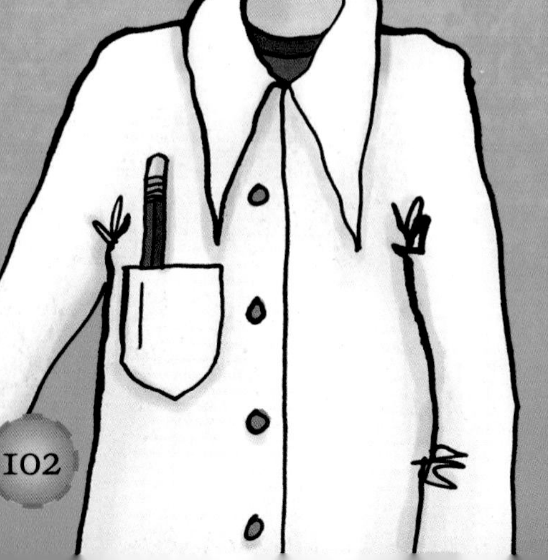

SUBSTANCES TO TRY:

- Vinegar
- Lemon juice
- Bicarbonate of soda
- Toothpaste
- Fizzy drinks
- Washing-up liquid

WHAT'S GOING ON?

This experiment is a way of finding out if a substance is an acid, or the opposite of an acid, an alkali. When an acid mixes with the red cabbage liquid, it reacts and changes colour, becoming more red. Alkalis make the liquid more blue. This kind of test is called a litmus test.

TROUBLESHOOTER

Use cups that are clear or plain white, so you can see the colour of the liquid clearly.

OUCH!

Bee and ant stings contain a type of acid, while wasp stings contain an alkali. Both types of chemical are painful when they get under your skin!

WHAT NEXT?

What else can you think of to test? Can you change the colour of the liquid using one substance, then change it back again using another?

Exploding drinks

This explosion isn't actually a chemical reaction, though it looks like one. You need to do this outdoors!

WHAT'S GOING ON?

The drink froths and foams, or even shoots out of the bottle, because of the carbon dioxide gas it contains. Normally, when you open a fizzy drink, the gas bubbles come out slowly. But the rough surface of the sweets helps the gas to separate from the water, and form big bubbles very fast. They can't all fit in the bottle, so the foamy liquid splurges out.

TROUBLESHOOTER

If you can't get a diet drink, a normal fizzy drink will also work, though the sugar may slow down the effect slightly.

DISSOLVING

When a fizzy drink is in its bottle with the lid on, the carbon dioxide gas is dissolved in it. This means it is broken into tiny bits and mixed into the drink. Solids can be dissolved too. For example if you stir sugar into tea, it dissolves. You can't see it, but it's still there.

WHAT NEXT?

What happens if you crush or break up the sweets first? Does it work better?

Does the experiment work if you put in other things, like a spoonful of salt, sugar or sand?

Make salt disappear and reappear

Salt dissolves easily in water, becoming invisible. You can make it reappear by making a crystal.

Here's What to Do...

1. Ask an adult to heat the pan of water and stir in and dissolve as much salt as possible.

2. They should let the water cool, then carefully pour the salty water into the jug, leaving any undissolved salt in the pan.

You can't see the salt, but you can taste a tiny bit of the water to check it's there.

3. Pour a little salty water onto the saucer, and leave it somewhere warm. The water will slowly dry up, leaving little square salt crystals.

4. Tie a piece of string to a pencil, wet the string and roll it in the salt crystals. Balance the pencil across the jug with the string dangling into the water, and leave it somewhere safe.

WHAT'S GOING ON?

When salt is stirred into hot water, it dissolves. But the salt is still there, waiting to form back into crystals. When the water dries up, or evaporates, bits of salt are left behind. When you put salt crystals on the string in the salty water, more and more salt sticks to them, growing a bigger and bigger crystal.

Salty water is all around us – in the sea, in foods such as cans of tuna and sweetcorn, even in our blood and body organs where it's essential for life.

WHAT NEXT?

Precious stones are crystals too. Crystals form and grow in regular shapes, like cubes or hexagons.

Can you find any other crystals in your home?

Rubbery bones

Bones are hard and stiff – that's how they hold us up. So how can you change a hard bone into a rubbery, bendy one?

Here's What to Do...

YOU WILL NEED

1) A chicken leg bone, saved from a roast chicken or drumstick
2) White vinegar
3) A food container with a lid
4) Kitchen paper

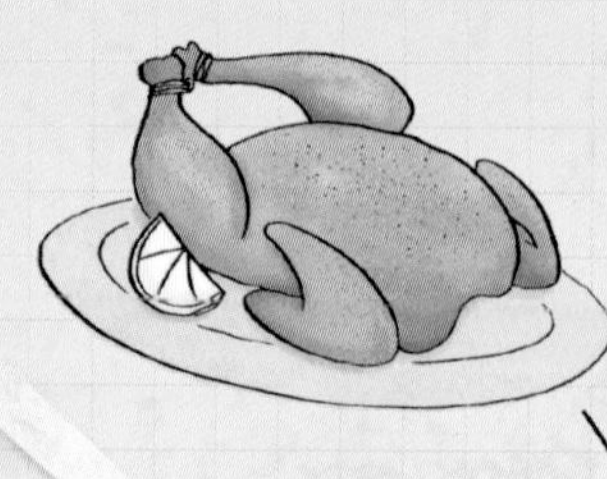

1. Pick all the meat off the chicken bone and wash it carefully. Can you bend it at all?

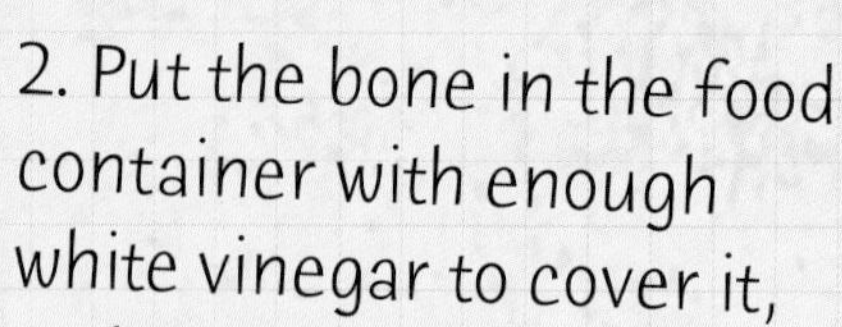

2. Put the bone in the food container with enough white vinegar to cover it, and put the lid on.

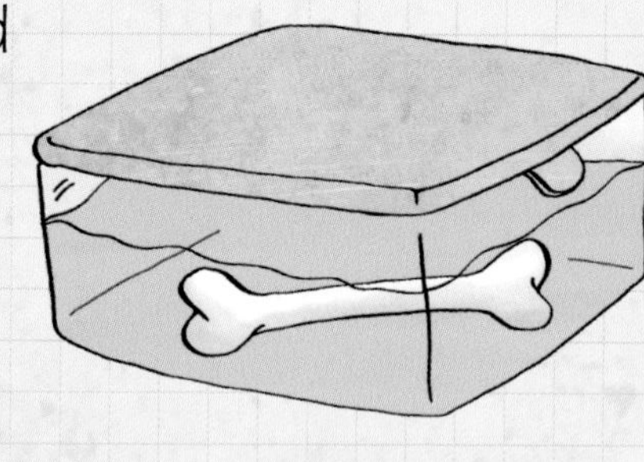

3. Leave it in a safe place for 5 days.

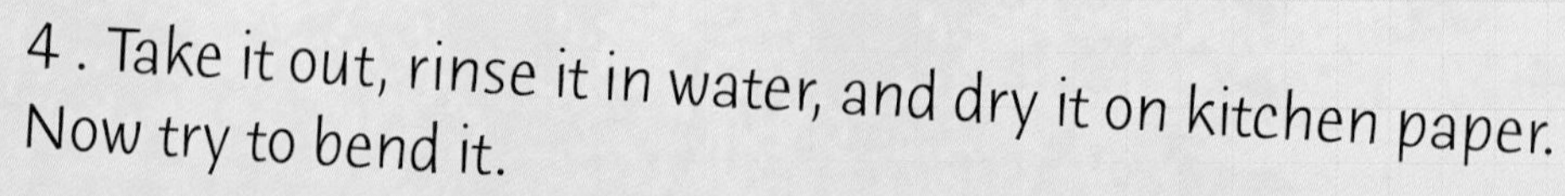

4 . Take it out, rinse it in water, and dry it on kitchen paper. Now try to bend it.

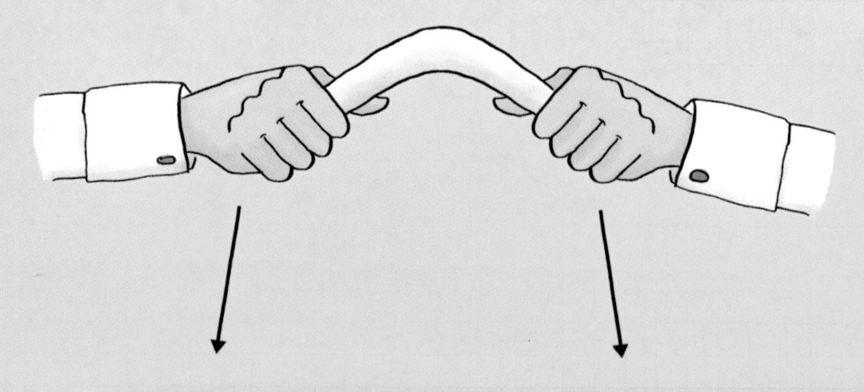

WHAT'S GOING ON?

The reason bones are hard is because they contain hard minerals – especially a substance called calcium, which is also found in many types of rock. Vinegar, a type of acid, is very good at dissolving calcium. As the vinegar soaks into the chicken bone, it dissolves the calcium, leaving a softer substance, known as collagen.

TROUBLESHOOTER

You can use dark-coloured vinegar if that's all you have – it's just a bit messier.

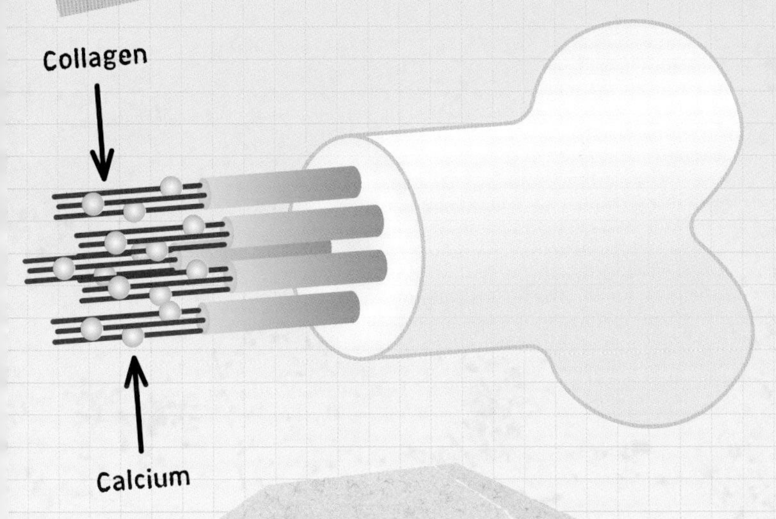

BENDY BONES

Part of your skeleton, including the tip of your nose and the joints in your back, are made of a bendy substance called cartilage, instead of bone. This helps some parts of our bodies to be more flexible. A shark's skeleton is all made of cartilage, to help it twist and bend in the water.

WHAT NEXT?

Can you actually tie your chicken bone in a knot?

Are any parts of your skeleton bendy and not hard? Try wiggling the tip of your nose.

Bottle balloon

Things also change when they heat up and cool down. One thing they do is get bigger and smaller.

YOU WILL NEED

1) A balloon
2) A medium-sized, empty plastic drinks bottle
3) A cold fridge
4) A warm radiator or sunny windowsill

Here's What to Do...

1. Stretch the opening of the uninflated balloon over the neck of the bottle.

2. Put the bottle and balloon in the fridge for a few minutes. What happens?

3. Take them out and stand the bottle somewhere warm, like on top of a radiator or on a sunny windowsill. What happens?

WHAT'S GOING ON?

Air is made up of gases. The gases are made of tiny molecules zooming around and crashing into each other. When a gas warms up, its molecules move faster and hit each other harder. This makes them spread out more and expand, taking up more space, and expanding the balloon. When air cools down, the molecules get slower and closer together, and the gas contracts, or shrinks.

In warm air, the molecules are further apart, so the air is lighter than cold air. This is why hot air balloons and paper fire lanterns float.

Most solids and liquids also get bigger as they get warmer, and smaller as they get cooler.

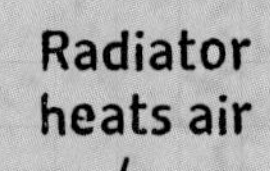

Radiator heats air

TROUBLESHOOTER

If the fridge doesn't make a big difference, try the freezer, or stand the bottle in a bowl of ice.

WHAT NEXT?

Try this experiment with a glass bottle. Wet the opening of the bottle with water and put a wet coin over the top. Hold the bottle in warm hands, or stand it on a radiator, to warm up the air inside. The expanding air will push the coin and make it jump.

Magic ice cubes

This experiment also works as a magic trick! Challenge your friends to pick up an ice cube with a piece of string and some salt, without touching it.

YOU WILL NEED

1) Several ice cubes
2) A bowl
3) Water
4) String
5) Table salt

Here's What to Do...

1. Fill the bowl with water and put in a few ice cubes. Can your friends get them out using the string? It's tricky!

2. To do it, dip the string in the water then lie it across the tops of the ice cubes.

3. Then sprinkle salt all over the ice cubes, and wait 30–60 seconds.

4. Now lift one end of the string. It should be stuck to the ice cubes and will pick them up.

WHAT'S GOING ON?

Water freezes into ice at freezing temperature, 0°Celsius. However, salty water freezes at a lower temperature. When salt touches the ice cubes, it makes a layer of salty water which is not cold enough to freeze, so the surface of the ice cube melts a little, and the string soaks into it. Then, the salt gradually flows away and the ice cubes freeze at 0°C again, holding the string beneath ice.

TROUBLESHOOTER

Rough parcel string works well – avoid very smooth string.

STRANGE WATER

Usually, substances always shrink as they get colder. But when water freezes into ice, its molecules push apart, and it actually expands a little. This means ice is less dense (heavy for its size) than water, and floats.

WHAT NEXT?

Does it work with a toothpick or lolly stick?

Can you work out why putting salt on icy roads makes them safer?

Plastic bag ice cream

You can make ice cream in a few minutes with ice, salt and a bit of shaking!

YOU WILL NEED

1) Full-fat milk
2) Sugar
3) Vanilla essence
4) Sealable sandwich bags
5) A larger plastic shopping bag or food bag
6) A large bag or several trays of ice cubes
7) A large packet of table salt or rock salt

Here's What to Do...

1. Put 250 ml (one cup) of milk, 4 teaspoons of sugar and a few drops of vanilla essence into a sandwich bag and seal it shut.

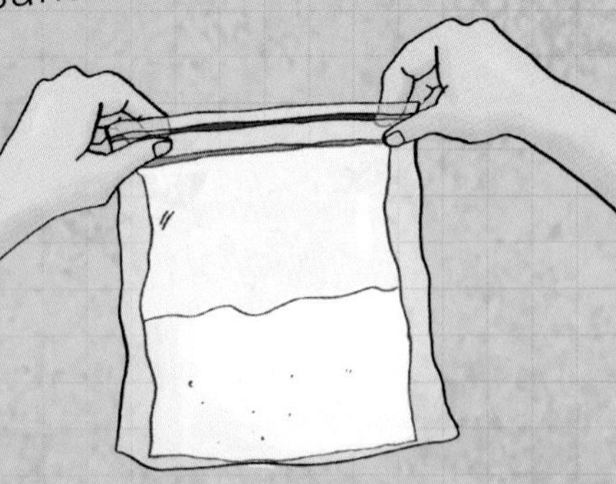

2. Put this bag inside a second sandwich bag and seal it shut, to protect against leaks.

3. Fill the larger bag with ice cubes, and mix in a large handful of salt.

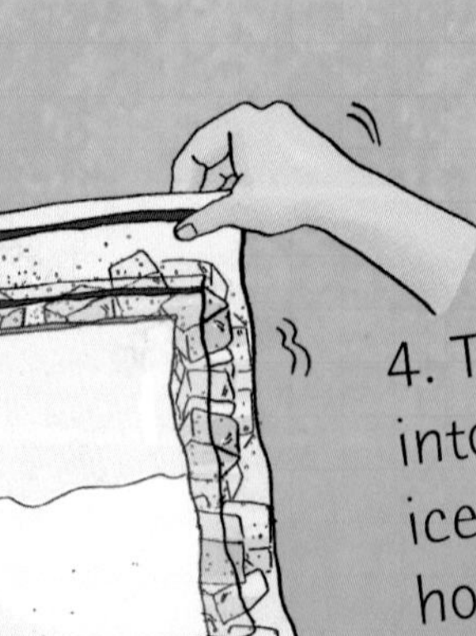

4. Tuck the bag of milk into the middle of the ice and salt mixture, hold it closed, and shake the whole bag for 5 minutes. Then take out your ice cream!

WHAT'S GOING ON?

The salt lowers the freezing temperature of the ice, making it start to melt. Melting takes energy, which sucks heat out of the bag of milk, and it freezes into ice cream.

TROUBLESHOOTER

Rock salt for de-icing pavements is best of all, if you have any, but other salt works too. Wipe the ice cream bag when you get it out to make sure no salt gets in.

QUICK SHAKE!

To make smooth, creamy ice cream, you have to freeze it fast and keep it moving. You do this by shaking, mixing or churning it in a machine. This helps to mix in a little air and keep the ice crystals small, so it isn't too hard and crunchy.

Factories use machines to make soft, smooth ice cream.

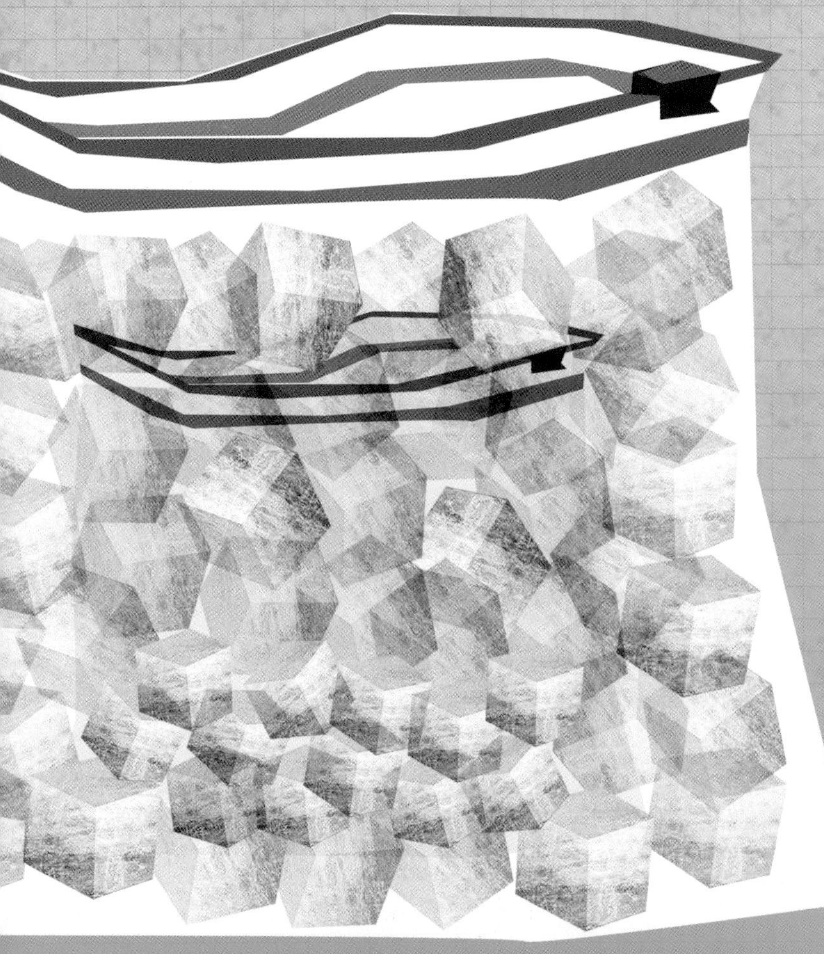

WHAT NEXT?

Once you can make ice cream, try different flavours instead of vanilla. See if it works with mint essence, banana milk powder or choc chips!

Pure water still

A still is a way to separate water from things that are mixed into it, such as dissolved salt.

YOU WILL NEED

1) Warm tap water
2) Table salt
3) A heatproof bowl
4) A small glass
5) Clingfilm or plastic food wrap
6) Sticky tape
7) A coin

Here's What to Do...

1. Half-fill the bowl with warm water and stir in several tablespoonfuls of salt until it dissolves. Taste a tiny bit of the water to check it is salty.

2. Stand the empty glass or jug in the bowl – it should be lower than the edge of the bowl, but taller than the water level.

3. Spread a piece of clingfilm or food wrap tightly over the bowl. Tape it in place if it won't stick.

4. Put the coin in the middle of the clingfilm, right over the empty glass.

5. Now carefully put the still somewhere warm, like on a windowsill in bright sunshine.

WHAT'S GOING ON?

After a while, you should end up with some clear water in the glass. Taste it to see if the salt is gone. Heat makes the water start to evaporate – change into a gas (called water vapour) – leaving the salt behind. The water vapour gets trapped under the plastic film, where it condenses – turns back into a liquid. Because the coin is weighing the plastic down in the middle, the water droplets run down the underside of the plastic film and drip into the glass.

In hot jungles, the air is damp because water vapour evaporates from the leaves of plants.

TROUBLESHOOTER

If it's not sunny, it should still work in a warm room, just a bit more slowly.

CHANGING TO A GAS

Water changes into water vapour at boiling temperature, 100°C. But it also evaporates slowly at lower temperatures. That's why puddles dry in the sun and washing dries on a line.

WHAT NEXT?

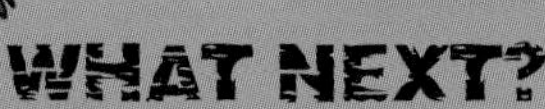

Try the experiment with water with food colouring in it, or with milk or squash. Does it work?

Make your own butter

Butter is made from cream – but how does liquid cream change into solid butter? You need to shake it.

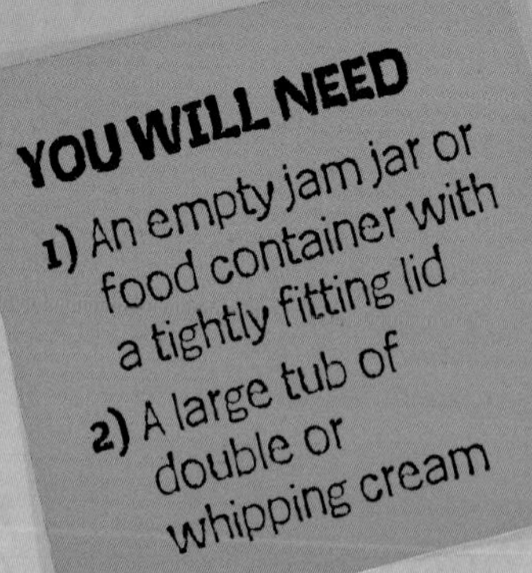

Here's What to Do...

1. Make sure your jar or container is completely clean and dry.

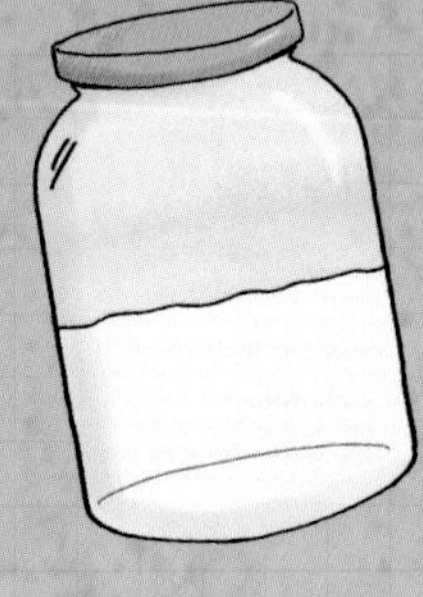

2. Half-fill it with cream and put the lid on tightly.

3. Now shake it – up and down, to and fro, and round and round. Take turns with friends or family if your arms get tired!

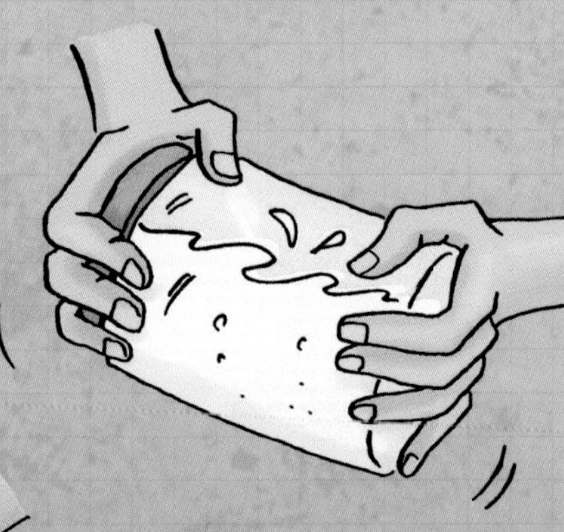

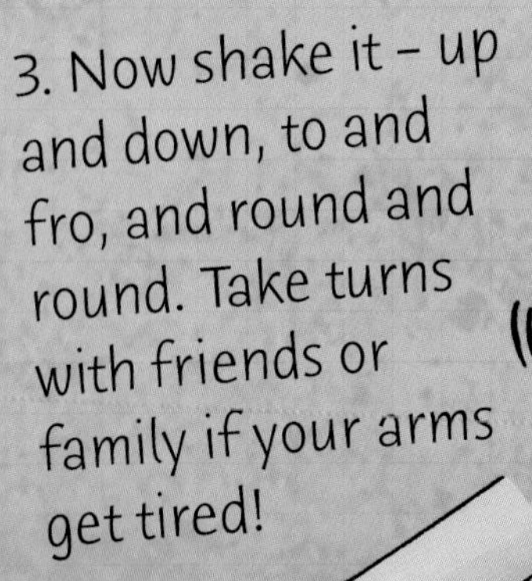

4. After around 10 minutes of shaking you should hear a slapping sound. This means the cream has changed into butter and watery buttermilk.

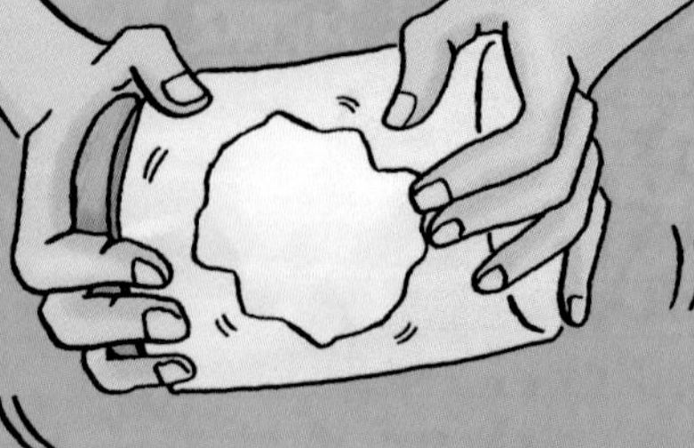

5. Pour away the buttermilk and rinse your butter in cold water a few times, then dry it in kitchen paper. It's ready to spread on a cracker and eat!

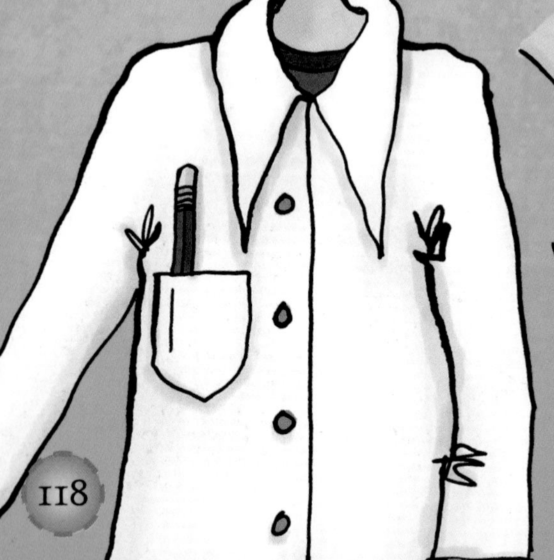

WHAT'S GOING ON?

Cream is a type of substance called an emulsion. It's made of watery liquid with tiny droplets of fat in it. Shaking makes the flat droplets bump and stick together. The more you shake, the more they stick until you have a big lump of fat (the butter) separated from the liquid (buttermilk).

TROUBLESHOOTER

It works best if the cream is room temperature, so leave it out of the fridge for a bit first if possible.

BUTTER CHURNS

Most butter is made in factories, by spinning cream around in a churning machine, which looks like a giant washing machine. Before machines, people used butter churns, wooden barrels which they had to turn or shake by hand.

WHAT NEXT?

Does it work with other types of cream, or full-fat milk?

Can you use your butter to make something else, like a cake?

Mould garden

If you leave an apple in the fruit bowl or bread in the bread bin for too long, it will turn mouldy and change into something disgusting. But why?

YOU WILL NEED

1) A clear glass jar with a tight lid, that you don't mind throwing away
2) Water
3) Glue
4) Sticky tape
5) Leftover food: try fruit, vegetables, bread, cake and cheese

Here's What to Do...

1. Make sure your jar is clean inside and the lid fits tightly.

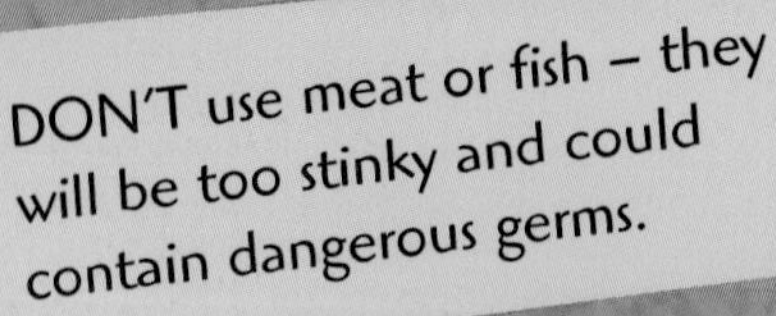

2. Wet a few pieces of food with water and put them into the jar, side by side.

DON'T use meat or fish – they will be too stinky and could contain dangerous germs.

3. Put glue around the top of the jar, put the lid on tightly and seal it with tape.

4. Put the jar in a safe place and check it every day to see what happens.

DON'T open the jar! – it will let mould out. Throw it away after a few days.

WHAT'S GOING ON?

As the food goes mouldy, it may grow furry blobs or white or green patches, and start to collapse. Moulds are a type of fungi, living things related to mushrooms. They spread by releasing spores, like tiny seeds, into the air. These land on food and eventually start growing and feeding on it. Normally, we eat food or throw it away before mould can grow.

Mould under a microscope.

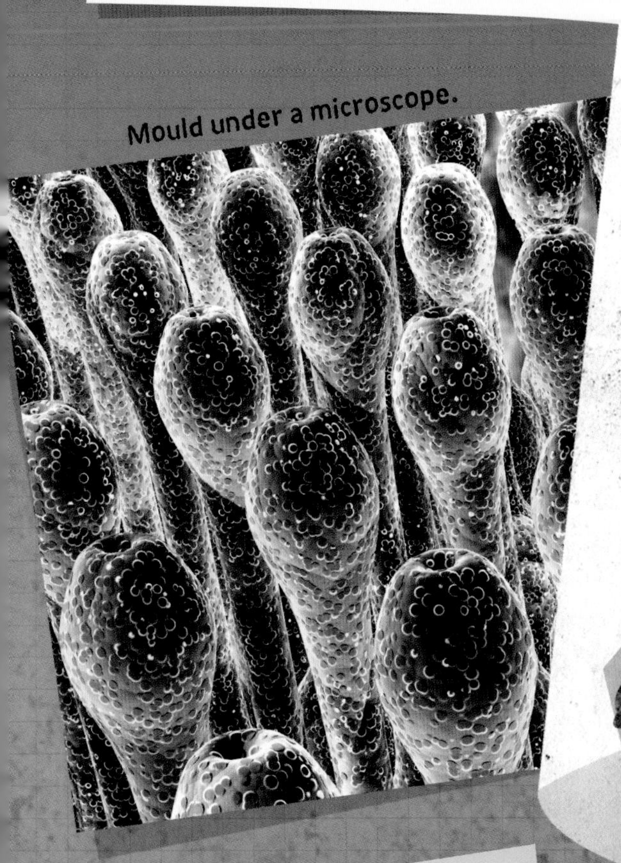

USEFUL MOULD

We use some types of mould to make medicines, and the 'veins' in blue cheese are also made of mould!

WHAT NEXT?

Can you take a photo of the jar at the same time every day to record what happens? You can put the photos together at the end to make a time-lapse sequence of the mould growing.

Make it
SPLASH!

SPLASH!

In everyday life, we're surrounded by liquids all the time. Water falls on our heads as rain, makes up most of our drinks, and fills our rivers and lakes, baths and swimming pools. Then there's runny paint and glue, cooking oil, and the liquid fuels that make cars and aircraft work.

LIKE WHAT?

Along with solids and gases, liquids are one of the three states of matter – forms that substances can exist in depending on how hot or cold they are. For example, on our planet, water is usually found as a liquid, but it can also be a solid (ice), and a gas (water vapour), which is found in the air.

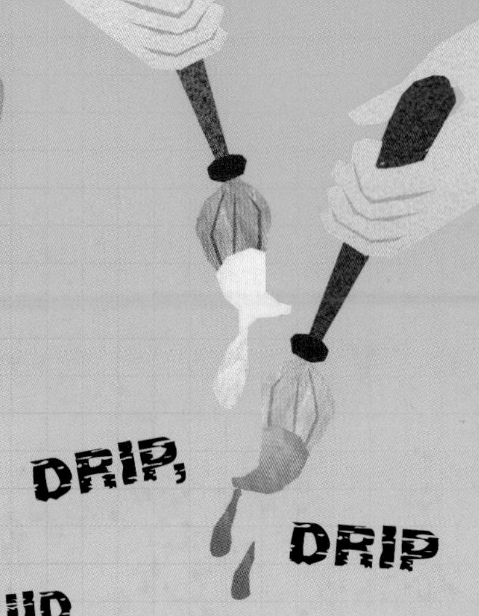

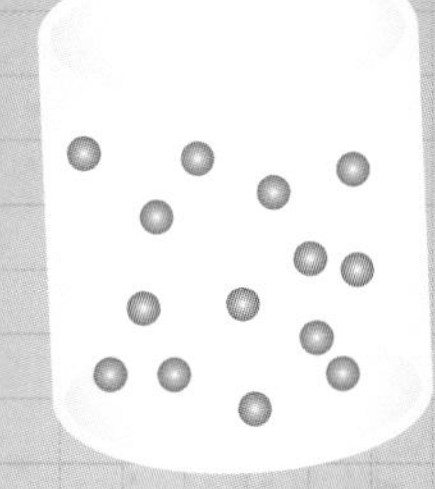

Solid Liquid Gas

LIKE A LIQUID

Liquids can do things that solids and gases can't. Solids tend to stay the same shape. Gases spread out to fill the space they are in. But a liquid moves in a different way. You can pour a liquid, make waves in it, or paint with it. Liquids can flow, spill, squirt, soak and SPLASH!

WATER OF LIFE

For us, water is the most important liquid of all. Living things need liquid water to survive. In fact, we exist because the Earth is mostly at the right temperature for water to exist as a liquid.

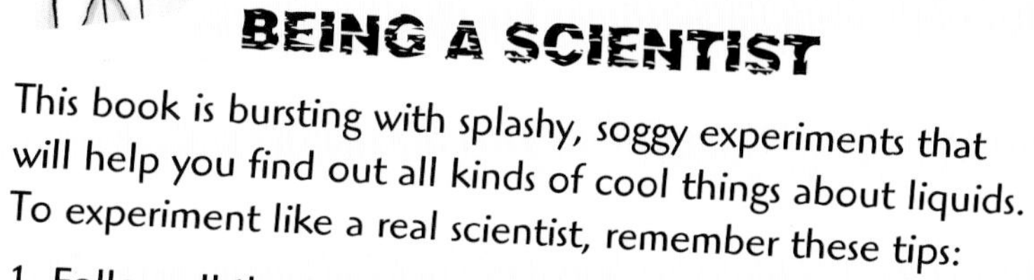

BEING A SCIENTIST

This book is bursting with splashy, soggy experiments that will help you find out all kinds of cool things about liquids. To experiment like a real scientist, remember these tips:

1. Follow all the instructions carefully.
2. Watch closely to see what happens, and try to record your results in writing or with photos.
3. If you can, do experiments more than once to see if they always work in the same way.

Make a Splash

Experiment with how liquids splash using these simple, yet messy tests. It might be best to do them outdoors!

YOU WILL NEED

1) A large bucket or washing-up bowl
2) Water
3) Waterproof household objects, like pebbles, buttons, coins or fruit
4) Small plastic bowls or yoghurt pots
5) Runny paint
6) Large pieces of plain paper or newspaper
7) A plastic cup
8) A tray

Here's What to Do...

1. Half-fill your bowl or bucket with water, and drop different objects into it. Which things make the biggest and smallest splashes?

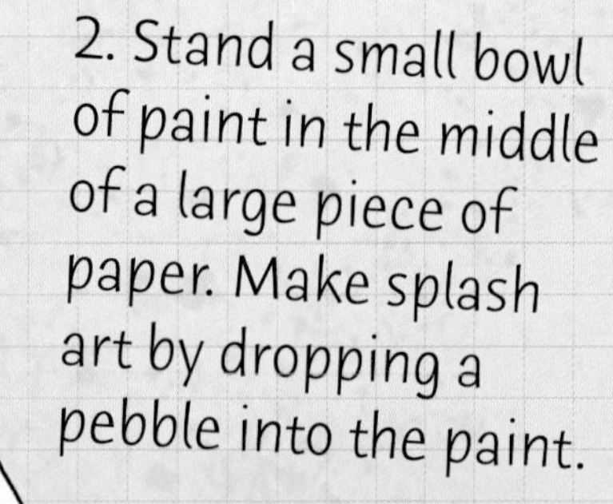

2. Stand a small bowl of paint in the middle of a large piece of paper. Make splash art by dropping a pebble into the paint.

3. Fill a plastic cup to the brim with water and stand it on a tray. Then hold the tray in one hand, stretch out your arm, and try walking a distance of 6 m without spilling any water.

WHAT'S GOING ON?

When you disturb a liquid, it moves around in waves and ripples, or separates into droplets – tiny 'pieces' of liquid. Droplets form a ball shape, because liquid likes to cling to itself. Heavier, lumpier objects make a bigger splash because they push more liquid out of the way. Light, smooth or thin objects make less of a splash, as they move less water.

TROUBLESHOOTER

If you do want to do these indoors, put down LOTS of newspaper or plastic mats and wear an apron.

PLOP!

See if you can capture a splash on video or as a freeze-frame photo.

WHAT NEXT?

Try test number three as a race with two or more friends, each with their own tray and cup. Who can keep the most water in their cup?

Stretchy water Skin

Why does water seem to have a stretchy skin?

WHAT'S GOING ON?

Water doesn't actually have a skin, but it seems to. This is because the molecules in water pull towards each other, especially at the surface. This makes a kind of stretchy barrier called surface tension. Soapy chemicals break the pull between the molecules, and destroy the surface tension.

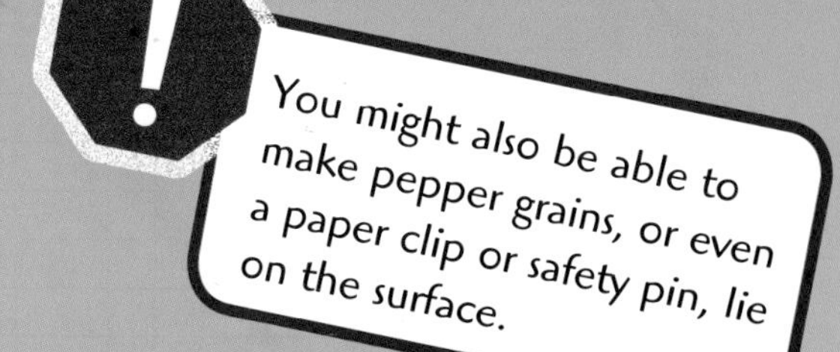

You might also be able to make pepper grains, or even a paper clip or safety pin, lie on the surface.

TROUBLESHOOTER

If you have trouble making things stay on the surface, try using tweezers to put them on, or lie them on a piece of tissue paper on the water. The paper will soak up water and sink, leaving the pins or needles behind.

Some water insects such as pond skaters and whirligig beetles use surface tension to skate along on top of the water.

WHAT NEXT?

Fill a small glass with water to the brim, then drop in pins to make it fuller and fuller. How many can you add before it overflows? Surface tension makes the water bulge out over the top of the glass.

Upside-down CUP

This experiment also makes an amazing magic trick! Do it outdoors or over a large water tray, just in case.

YOU WILL NEED

1) A handkerchief or any piece of thin fabric
2) A small glass
3) A jug of water

Here's What to Do...

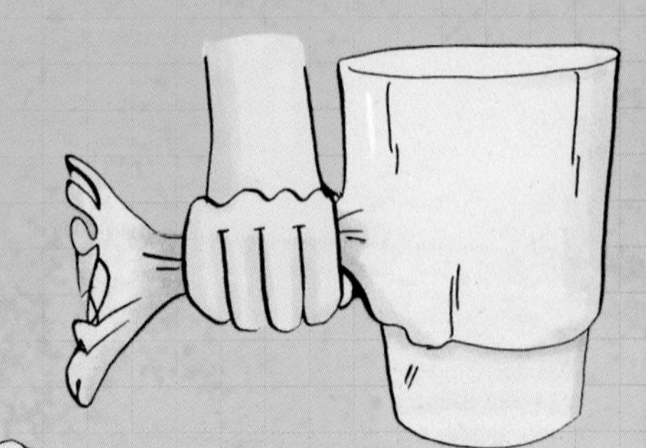

1. Put your handkerchief or fabric over the glass and hold it loosely in place.

2. Carefully pour water through the fabric into the glass, until it's almost full.

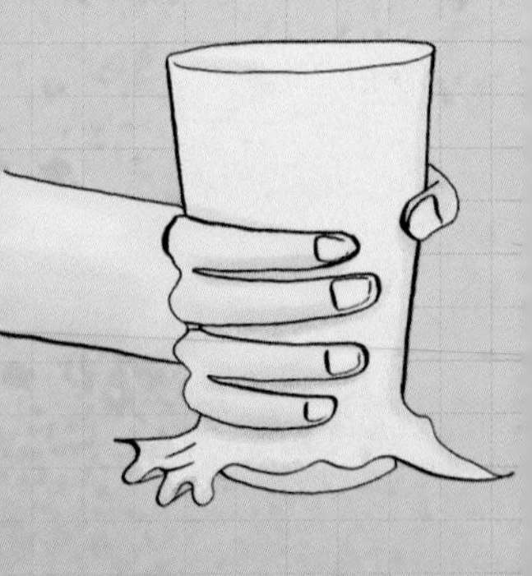

3. Put your hand around the glass and pull the fabric down so that it's stretched tightly across the top of the glass.

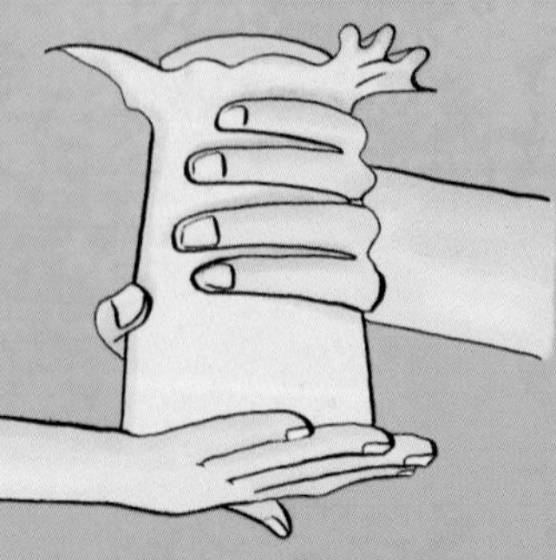

4. Put your other hand over the glass and turn it upside down.

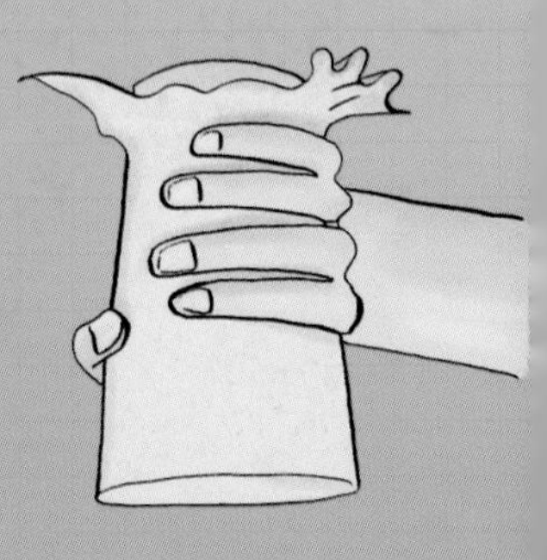

5. Then – ta-daa! – gently take your hand away. The water doesn't fall out!

WHAT'S GOING ON?

When the water is flowing and the fabric can move and ripple, the surface tension is broken and the water gets through. When the glass is upside down, the water's surface tension forms a barrier across each tiny hole in the smooth, flat, tightly stretched fabric.

TROUBLESHOOTER

The fabric must be stretched smooth and tight for it to work.

WATERPROOF SKIN

Tents and umbrellas often use surface tension to keep water out. When the fabric is stretched tight, it can get covered in rain, but the rain doesn't come through, even if the fabric isn't waterproof. Instead the surface tension makes the water 'block' all the tiny holes in the fabric.

WHAT NEXT?

You can do a similar trick by placing a postcard on top of a brim-full cup of water. Hold it on, turn the cup upside down, then let go. The card forms a barrier that doesn't let air in, so water can't fall out because there is no air to replace it.

Water balloon POP

If you fill a balloon with water, what does the water inside it look like? Find out by taking a photo! You need at least two people.

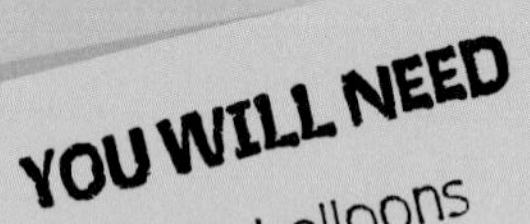

YOU WILL NEED

1) Party balloons
2) String
3) A pin or needle
4) A camera or cameraphone

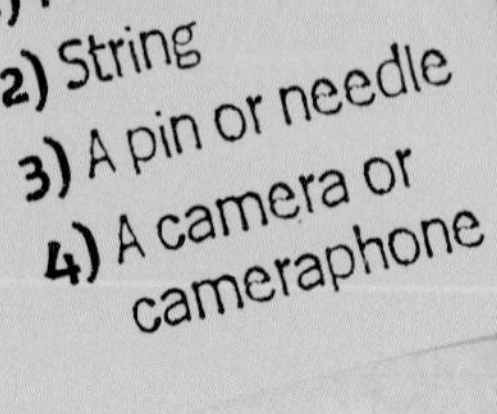

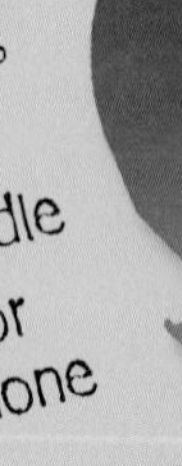

Here's What to Do...

1. Fill several party balloons with water and tie them closed.

2. Use string to hang the balloons up on a washing line, low tree branch or something similar, outdoors! If there's nothing suitable to hang them on, ask someone to stand and hold the string.

3. One person should pop a balloon with a pin.

4. At the moment of popping, another person should take a photo of the balloon. Use the fastest shutter speed possible or set the camera to 'action' mode.

WHAT'S GOING ON?

It may take a few tries to get a good photo (that's why you need several balloons!) – but if you're lucky you will capture a balloon-shaped ball of water hanging in mid-air after the balloon pops. The stretchy balloon skin shrinks so fast that it leaves the water uncovered before gravity pulls it to the ground.

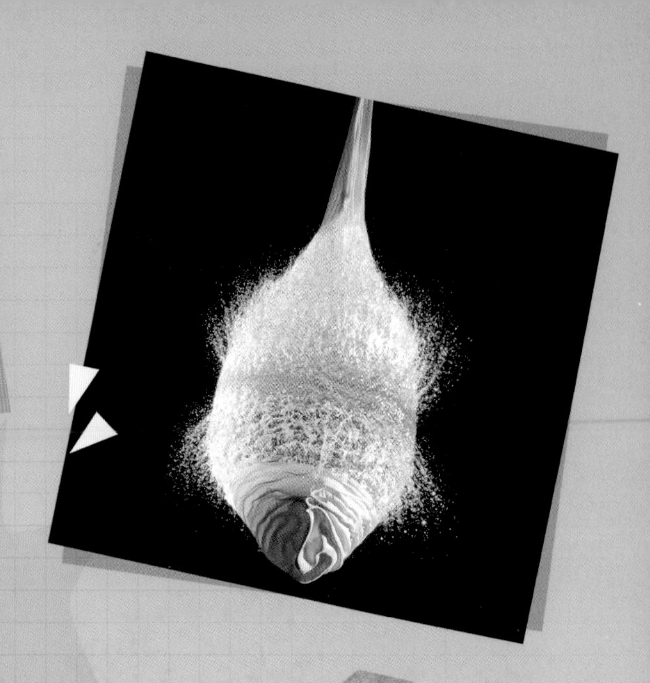

TROUBLESHOOTER

Count 3, 2, 1, pop! to get the timing as exact as possible.

SPACE BALLOON

Astronauts have also done this experiment in space, where it's easier to get a good look!

WHAT NEXT?

You could try videoing the pop, then playing back the film slowed down to see what happens. You could even ask someone to try to catch the water ball as it falls, for an extra splashy photo!

Things that float

Try this experiment to find out what things float in water, and why.

YOU WILL NEED

1) A large mixing or washing-up bowl
2) Water
3) A selection of everyday objects
4) Modelling clay

Here's What to Do...

1. Half-fill the large bowl with water.

2. Put different objects in it to see what floats and what doesn't.

OBJECTS TO TRY

Coin, paper clip, chocolate, seashell, pebble, cork, eraser, buttons, toys, balls, wooden pegs

Can you guess which ones will float before you put them in?

3. Make a round ball of modelling clay – it should sink.

4. Can you make the clay into a shape that floats, even though it is a material that sinks?

WHAT'S GOING ON?

Water can hold up any object that is less dense than itself. Density means how heavy an object is for its size. A coin is small and quite dense. It sinks because it is heavier than an amount of water of the same size and shape, and the water cannot hold it up. A cork is much less dense. It pushes down into the water a little, but the water can easily hold it up.

Modelling clay is dense and doesn't float. But if you make a boat or cup shape out of the clay, it does! This is because the shape now includes the air inside it. Taken together, the air and the clay make an object that is less dense than water.

BIG BOATS

Huge ocean ships are made of metal and are very heavy – but they float because of all the air inside them.

WHAT NEXT?

Can you find any natural boat shapes, such as bottle tops or fruit skins? See if they float.

Try to build a boat that moves – could you add a small sail and make wind by blowing through a straw?

Rising raisins

Amaze your friends with raisins that float, then sink, then float again!

YOU WILL NEED

1) A few raisins
2) Fizzy water or a clear fizzy drink, such as lemonade
3) A tall glass
4) A stopwatch

Here's What to Do...

1. Fill the glass with the fizzy drink, almost to the top.
2. Drop a raisin into the drink and watch it sink to the bottom.
3. Wait a minute or two. What happens?
4. How long will your raisin keep rising and sinking? See if you can time it.

WHAT'S GOING ON?

The raisin is denser than the drink, so at first it sinks. But as it sits in the fizzy liquid, gas bubbles from the drink start to get stuck to the raisin's rough surface. Eventually, it has so many bubbles on it that it becomes lighter and less dense, so it floats. But when it reaches the surface, the bubbles escape into the air. Without its bubbles, the raisin sinks back to the bottom – and the cycle begins again!

TROUBLESHOOTER

You need a really bubbly, freshly opened fizzy drink, not an old one.

FROM FIZZY TO FLAT

If you leave a fizzy drink in a glass, eventually all the gas bubbles will escape from it, and it will go 'flat'. Once this happens, the raisin will stop moving.

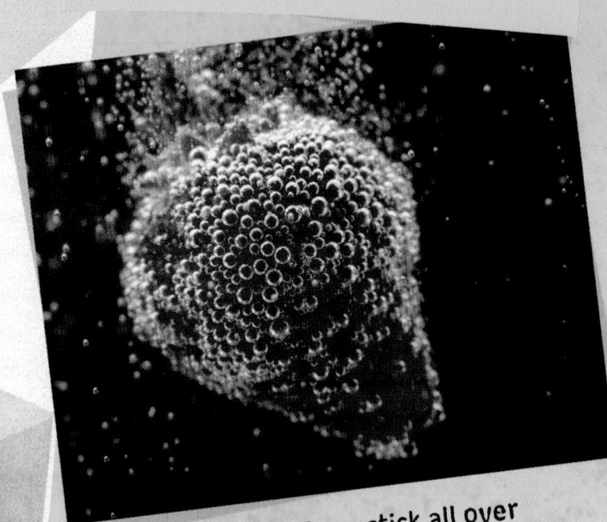

Bubbles of gas stick all over the surface of objects dropped into fizzy drinks.

WHAT NEXT?

Try the same experiment with other objects like popcorn, paper clips, small sweets or pasta shapes. Do any of them behave the same way? Do any of them stay at the bottom of the drink, or stay floating on the top? Do they get soggy?

Magic liquid levels

It's not just solid objects that float on liquids – other liquids do too.

YOU WILL NEED

1) A tall, clear glass, jam jar
2) A measuring jug
3) 6 paper cups
4) 100 ml (half a cup) each of runny honey, maple syrup, washing-up liquid, milk, cooking oil (such as sunflower oil) and water

Here's What to Do...

1. Measure out your six liquids into the six paper cups, using the measuring jug.

2. Pour the honey into the bottom of your jar.

3. Add the other liquids one by one, pouring them slowly and carefully into the middle so they don't stick to the sides.

4. Let the liquids settle. What happens?

WHAT'S GOING ON?

As you pour them in, the densest liquids sink down, and the less dense liquids rise up and float on top of them, creating a stripy tower of different layers. Scientists call this a density column.

TROUBLESHOOTER

Try to choose liquids of different colours, such as bright pink or green washing-up liquid and golden honey. You could also add some food colouring to the water in the paper cup, to make it easier to see.

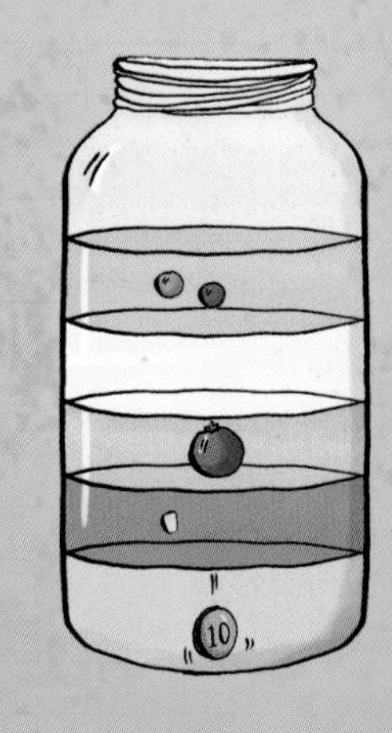

OIL ON WATER

Oil is less dense than water and floats on top of it. That's why oil spills at sea are bad news. The oil sits on the water surface, forming an oil slick, and making water birds' feathers dirty and sticky.

WHAT NEXT?

Now try dropping in some small objects to see if they float on top, sink to the bottom or stop somewhere in the middle. Try a coin, popcorn kernel or sunflower seed, a plastic bead, a small tomato or a toy brick.

Melting Crayon art

Solids can become liquids when they get hot and melt. You can sometimes see this happening with ice and snow, butter or chocolate – and in this experiment, wax crayons.

WHAT'S GOING ON?

When the crayons are solid they hold their shape. But when the heat melts them they become a liquid and start to flow, so gravity can pull them downwards. By tipping and tilting the card, you can make the wax flow into all kinds of crazy patterns.

Solid

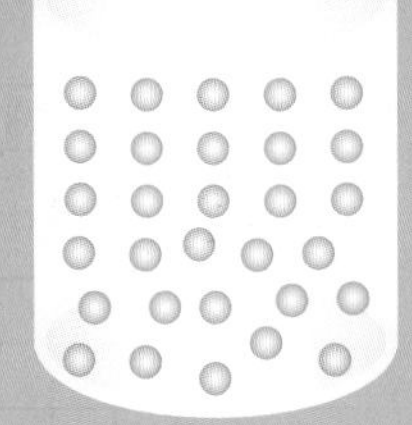
Solid/Liquid

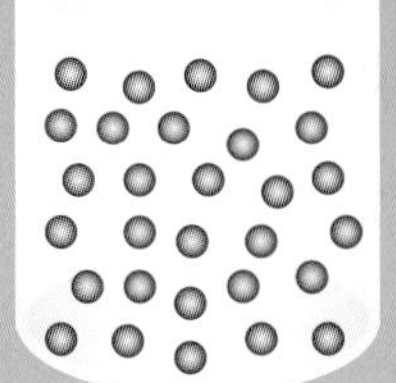
Liquid

The solid ice becomes a liquid, water, when it melts.

TROUBLESHOOTER

You can use brown card from a large cardboard box if you don't have white card.

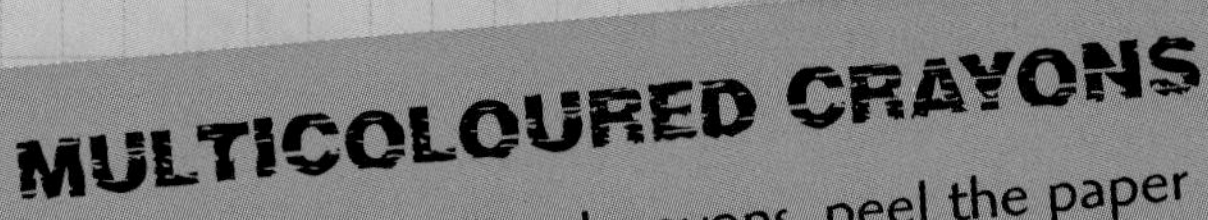

MULTICOLOURED CRAYONS

To make multicoloured crayons, peel the paper off a few crayons and put them in a paper cup. Heat the cup with the hairdryer until they have melted then swirl them together with a stick. Leave the mix to cool and harden, then pop out!

WHAT NEXT?

For a shiny version, cover your card with silver foil before you stick the crayons on.

The Saliva test

Did you know that food has to be dissolved in liquid before you can taste it? Try this test to find out how important your saliva (spit) is!

YOU WILL NEED

1) Some strong-tasting foods, such as salty crisps and sweet dried apricots, or a few grains of salt and sugar
2) Paper or plastic plates
3) Kitchen paper

1. Set out your foods on separate plates.

2. Stick your tongue out and dab a bit of each food onto it. You should be able to taste them straight away.

3. Now dry your tongue all over with kitchen paper.

4. Dab the foods on your tongue again. Is there any difference?

WHAT'S GOING ON?

Your tongue has taste-sensing taste buds in it, but they are in tiny cracks in the tongue's surface. For food to reach them, it has to be washed down into the cracks. Your tongue is normally wet because your mouth constantly releases saliva. As soon as the saliva touches food, it dissolves some of it and washes it down the gaps. When your tongue is totally dry, this can't happen and you can't taste anything.

TROUBLESHOOTER

You need to use foods that are quite dry, so avoid juicy fruit or yoghurt.

WE NEED SPIT

Saliva has other uses, too. It helps to make food mushy and soft, so it's easier to swallow. It can also kill some types of germs.

WHAT NEXT?

Chocolate is designed to stay solid until it's in your mouth, when it melts into a liquid. Try putting some squares of chocolate in the freezer, then compare them with unfrozen squares. What happens when you put them in your mouth? Can you taste the unfrozen squares sooner?

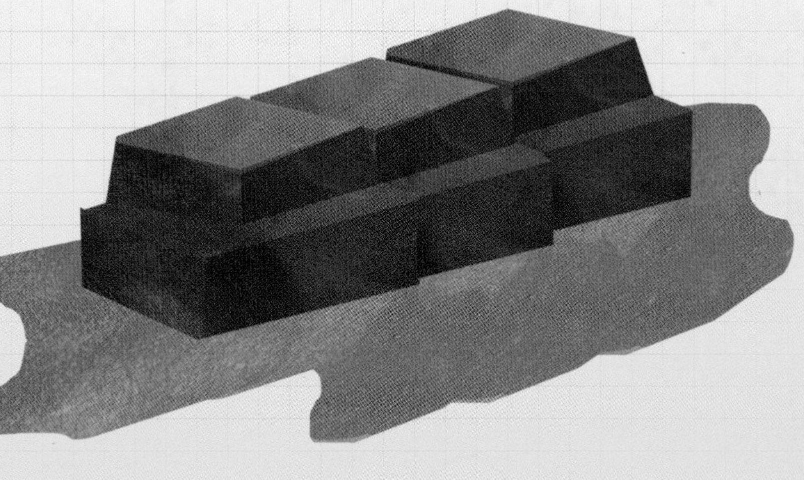

Make your own river

Though water seems soft, it can cut a path through sand, soil or solid rock. That's how rivers form.

YOU WILL NEED

1) Plenty of play sand (available at garden centres)
2) A large, shallow tray that can get wet and dirty
3) Pebbles of various sizes
4) A garden hose or a large jug of water

Here's What to Do...

1. Find somewhere safe outdoors to put the tray, where it's OK to spill water and sand.

2. Use the sand and a few pebbles to build a gently sloping hillside in the tray, with the top of the hill at one end. Pack the sand down firmly.

3. Use the garden hose or water jug to pour a slow, steady trickle of water onto the top of your hill.

4. Watch as the water finds its way downhill and carves itself a river bed.

WHAT'S GOING ON?

As gravity pulls the water downwards, it finds the easiest path, flowing around harder areas and blockages. As the water flows, it washes away some sand, creating a channel which gets bigger and bigger as more water flows along it.

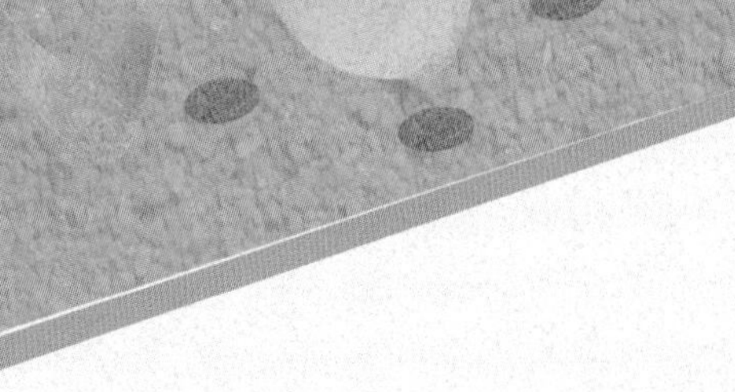

TROUBLESHOOTER

You want the water to flow away off the tray once it reaches the other end, so don't use a deep tray.

RIVERS AND ROCKS

Rivers cut through sand easily, but they can also wear through rock, though this takes much longer. The water gradually dissolves the rock as it flows along, and sand and pebbles carried along in the water also wear it away.

WHAT NEXT?

Look at maps or satellite pictures (for example, of the Nile in Egypt or the Irtysh River in Russia), or at other rivers next time you're in a high-up place or on board a plane, to see how their paths have formed.

You could also do this activity on a sandy beach without a tray. Just build a sandy, pebbly hill and pour water down it.

Strange gloop

Some strange liquids don't behave quite the way you expect! Do this experiment outside, or make sure you put down lots of newspaper.

YOU WILL NEED

1) A packet of cornflour, also called cornstarch or maize flour
2) A large mixing bowl
3) Water
4) A cup
5) A spoon

Here's What to Do...

1. Put about a cupful of cornflour into the bowl.

2. Stir in a cupful of cold water, adding a little at a time until you have a gloopy liquid as thick as runny honey.

3. If you gently stir, pour or swirl the mixture, it's runny like a normal liquid.

4. But what happens when you try to stir it quickly, or hit the surface hard with your hand?

WHAT'S GOING ON?

This mixture is called a non-Newtonian fluid, meaning it doesn't behave according to the normal laws of liquid science. When you are gentle with it, it flows and splashes. But when it's pushed hard, the particles in it jam together and form a lump, making it behave like a solid.

TROUBLESHOOTER

You may need to keep adding a little of both ingredients until you get the mixture just right.

HOLDING GLOOP

You might even be able to squeeze together a handful of the gloop into a ball, if you keep holding it tight. When you let go, it goes runny again!

WALKING ON GLOOP

Some experimenters have even tried filling a whole paddling pool with cornflour gloop to see if they could run across the surface. They could!

WHAT NEXT?

You can use a little green food colouring to turn your strange gloop into spooky slime!

More water fun

Not quite soaked through yet? Here are some more amazing water tricks to try!

YOU WILL NEED

1) Water
2) A garden hose or spray bottle with a fine mist setting
3) 2 paper cups
4) String
5) Strong sticky tape
6) A kitchen or bathroom tap
7) An assistant to help you

Here's What to Do...

1. Make a rainbow
On a sunny day, stand with the sun behind you and spray a fine mist of water using a garden hose or spray bottle. A rainbow should appear in the misty water cloud.

2. Walking water
Tape a piece of string to the inside of the paper cup and ask your assistant to hold the cup still. Hold the string so that it slopes up diagonally out of the cup. Fill the other cup with water and slowly pour it out onto the end of string. It should travel along the string into the empty cup.

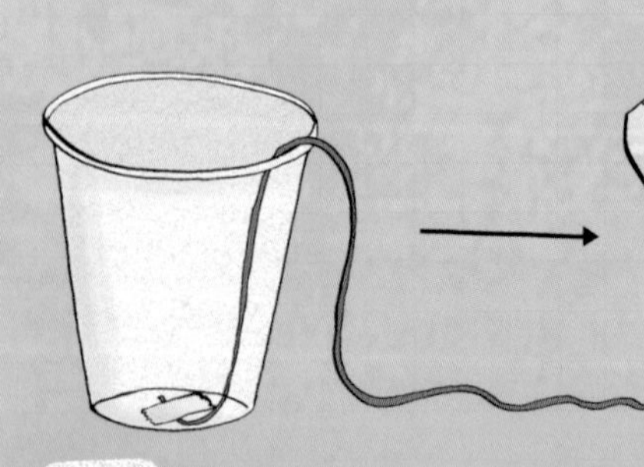

TROUBLESHOOTER

The string will work best if you wet it first, but keep one end dry for taping.

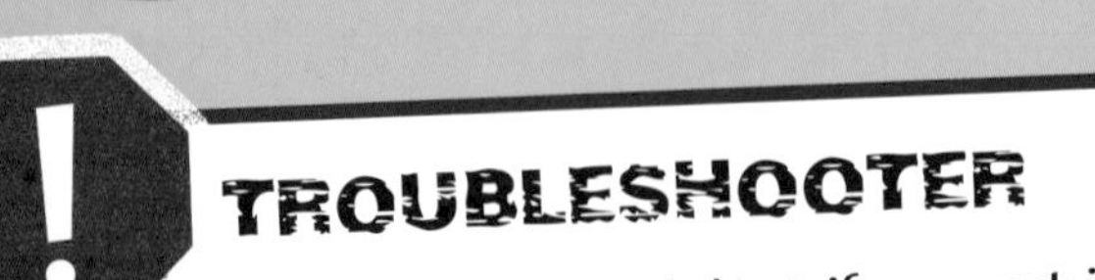

3. String of pearls

Turn on a tap so that it is making a very thin, straight flow of water. Put your finger under the flow and lift it up close to the tap. Can you make the water form a series of tiny sphere shapes?

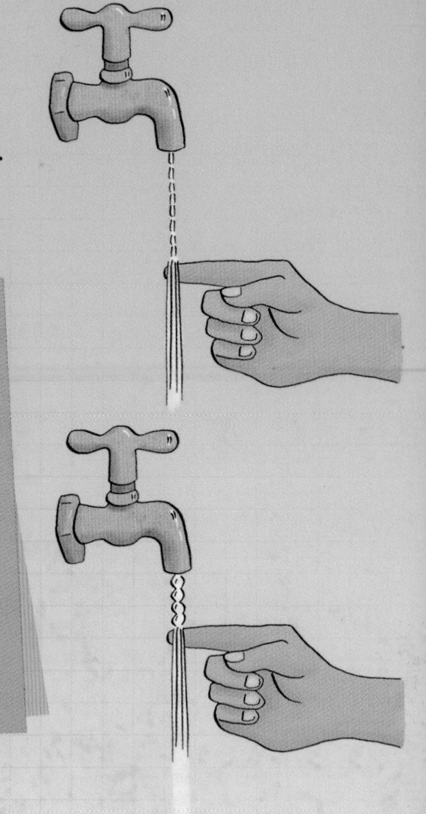

WHAT'S GOING ON?

The rainbow appears because as sunlight passes in and out of water droplets, it refracts or bends, and splits into separate colours.

The water 'walks' along the string because of a force called cohesion, which means sticking together. The water molecules cling to each other as they flow along the string, instead of dropping off it.

The string of pearls effect happens because there is such a small amount of water above your finger that surface tension tries to pull it into round droplets.

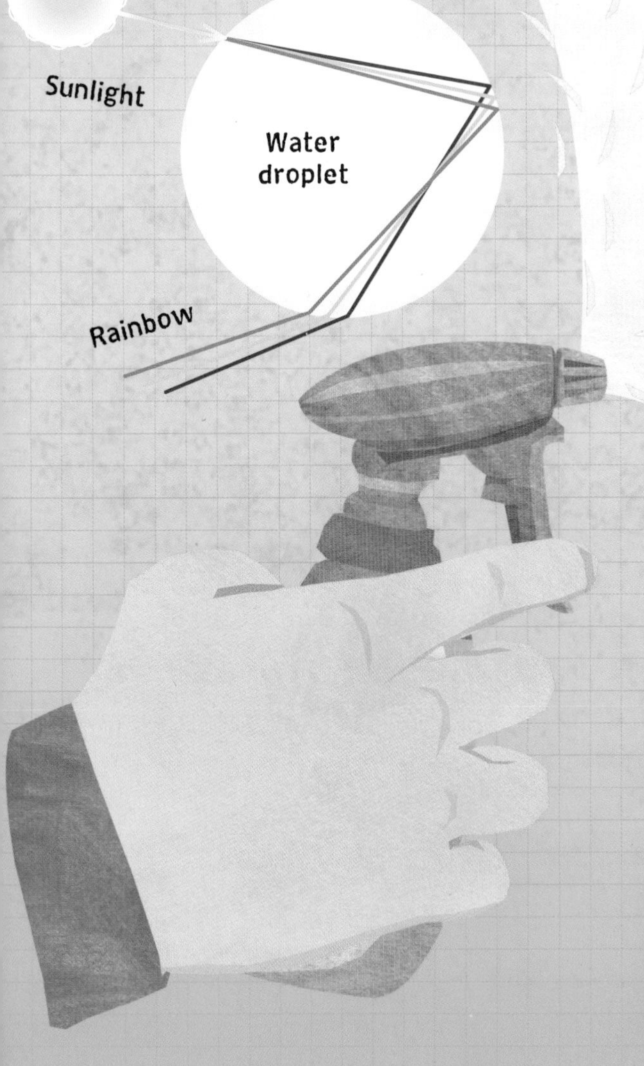

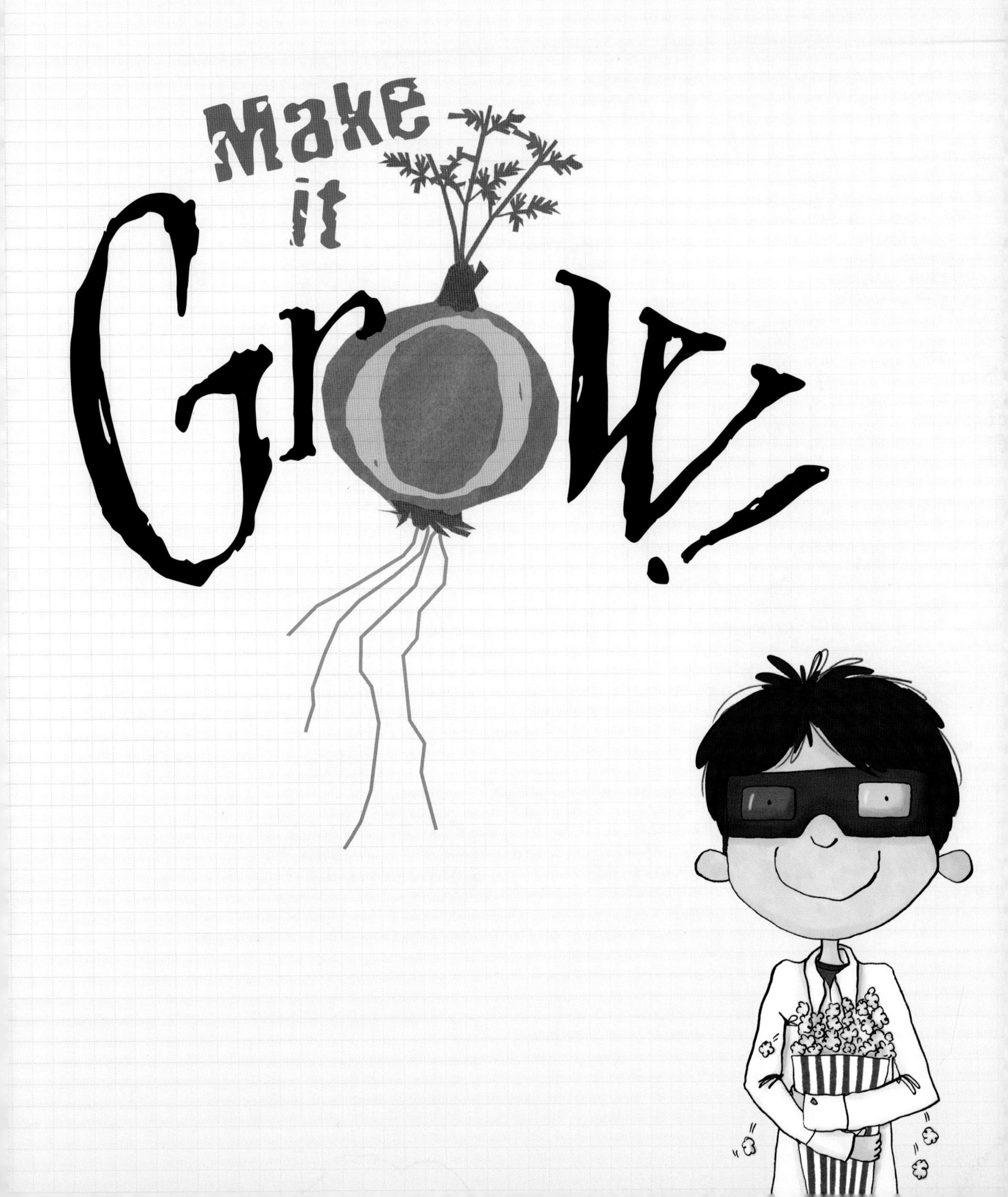
Make it Grow!

Bigger and BIGGER!

We're surrounded all the time by things that are growing and changing. Living things, such as plants, trees and animals all grow. You are a living thing too, and you are also growing.

LIKE WHAT?

Non-living things, such as crystals and clouds, can also grow. And although you may not always notice it, any substance can get bigger or smaller, depending on how hot or cold it is. In fact, there's hardly anything that stays the same size! Here are some examples:

- Storm clouds get bigger and change shape.
- A baby grows into a child, then an adult.
- Plants don't just grow taller, they also grow new buds, leaves or flowers every year.
- Air grows and takes up more space when it gets hotter.

TEST IT OUT

The activities in this book let you explore how things grow, and the different reasons why they do. You can experiment with plants, crystals, ice, hot air, and even try out some expanding food recipes that you can eat afterwards!

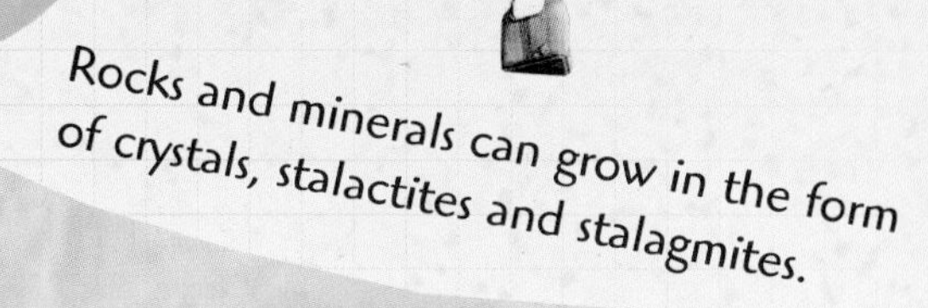
Rocks and minerals can grow in the form of crystals, stalactites and stalagmites.

BEING A SCIENTIST

When you do science experiments, you are finding out how the world works, just like a real scientist. To do it right, follow these real-life science tips:

1. Always follow the instructions and watch what happens carefully.
2. Write down the results to keep a record of them. You can also take photos or make sketches.
3. If possible, do experiments a few times over to check they always work.

Egg-head

Real hair grows, and so does this cress hair! Use it to make yourself a green-haired egg-head. You will need an adult to help you with the egg-boiling part.

YOU WILL NEED

1) A fresh egg
2) A saucepan
3) A cooker
4) Water
5) Felt-tip pens
6) Kitchen paper
7) Cotton wool
8) Cress seeds

Here's What to Do...

1. Ask an adult to hard-boil the egg and let it cool. Then slice the top off, eat (or throw away) the egg and carefully wash out and dry the shell.

2. Draw a face on your eggshell.

3. Put a piece of wet kitchen paper in the bottom of the shell, and a ball of wet cotton wool on top.

4. Sprinkle cress seeds onto the cotton wool. Stand it in a warm, sunny place such as a windowsill.

WHAT'S GOING ON?

It will take a couple of days, but your cress seeds should start to sprout and grow. They don't need soil, just water, warmth and light. Seeds can sense when they have the things they need to grow, and this makes them start to sprout, or germinate.

A seed sends roots down into the soil and a shoot grows upwards.

TROUBLESHOOTER

To help your egg-head stand up, you can sit it in an egg cup or egg box, or on top of a toilet roll tube.

If you don't want to use an egg, a small yoghurt pot or plant pot works too.

TIME FOR LUNCH!

When the cress has grown, you can eat it (unlike real hair!). Snip it off at the bottoms of the stalks, wash it, and put it in a salad or an egg or cheese sandwich.

WHAT NEXT?

You can keep your cress head extra warm and damp by covering it with a mini 'greenhouse' made of an upside-down clear plastic bowl.

Growing beans

A seed contains all the information it needs to grow into a plant, as long as it gets the right things. What will make it keep growing? Runner bean or green bean seeds are best for this.

YOU WILL NEED

1) Two empty glass jam jars
2) Runner bean or green bean seeds from a garden centre
3) Kitchen paper
4) Water
5) A large cardboard box with lid flaps

Here's What to Do...

1. Line each jar with a piece of kitchen paper, curving it around the inside like this.

2. Push two beans halfway down inside each jar between the glass and the paper.

3. Add about 4 cm of water to each jar, making sure it touches the bottom of the kitchen paper.

4. Leave one jar on a sunny windowsill. Put the other next to it, but inside a cardboard box with the lid flaps closed.

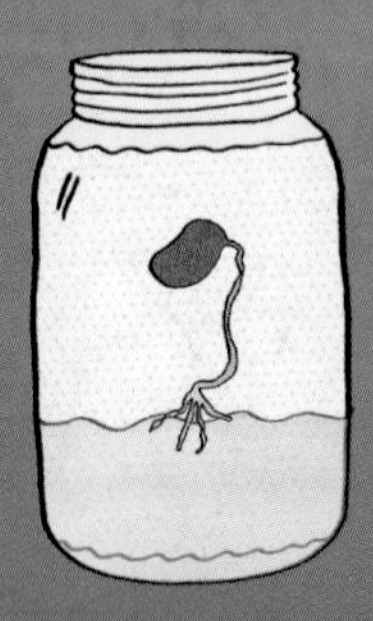

?

5. Check every day to see what's happening!

WHAT'S GOING ON?

The seeds should germinate and sprout a stalk and a root. But to keep growing bigger and bigger, plants need light, so the one in the dark may not do as well.

TROUBLESHOOTER

To stop the paper and seeds from drying out, top up the water level each day.

WHY DO PLANTS NEED LIGHT?

Plants grow by turning water and carbon dioxide gas from the air into sugary food. This process, called photosynthesis, uses energy. Plants get this energy by taking in light through their leaves. A seed can start to grow using food energy stored inside it, but can't carry on for long without light.

WHAT NEXT?

A bean seed that's growing well can be moved into a pot of soil and then planted in a sunny place or container outdoors. With luck you should be able to grow beans to eat.

Supermarket Sprout

You might have noticed vegetables in your fridge or cupboards starting to 'sprout' when they get a bit old. This experiment lets you take a closer look at what happens. Compare non-organic vegetables with organic ones, to see if there's a difference.

YOU WILL NEED

1) Organic and non-organic potatoes, onions and carrots
An empty egg box
2) An empty egg box
3) Small glasses, jars and saucers
4) Water

Here's What to Do...

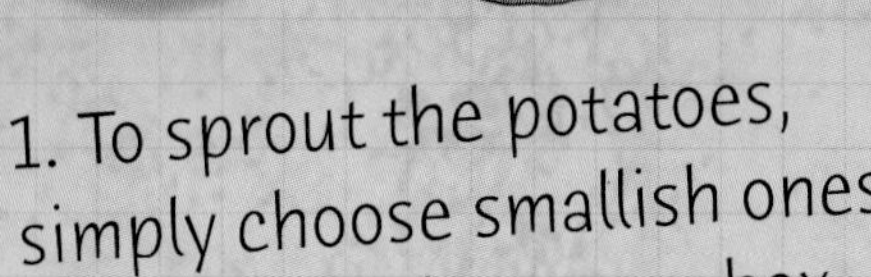

1. To sprout the potatoes, simply choose smallish ones and sit them in an egg box.

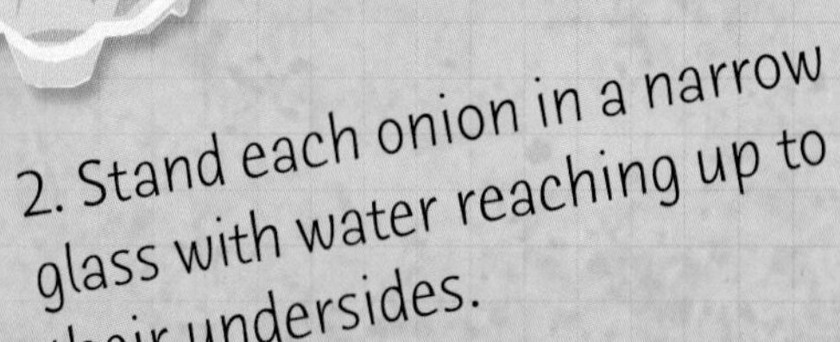

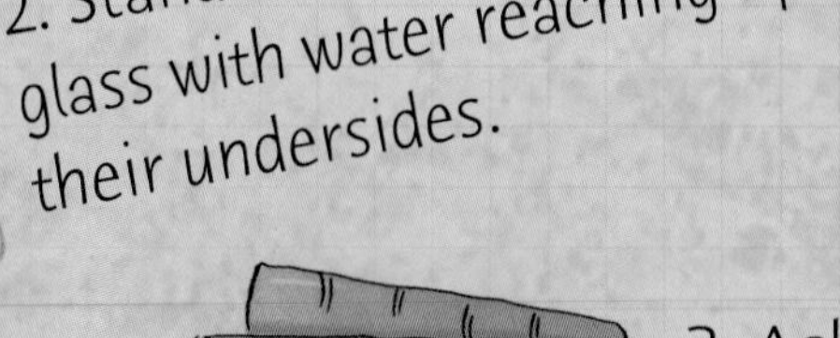

2. Stand each onion in a narrow glass with water reaching up to their undersides.

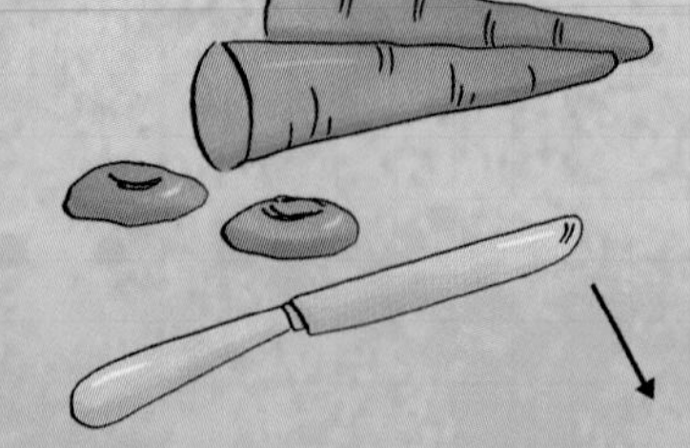

3. Ask an adult to cut off the thick ends of the carrots and stand them in saucers of water.

4. Leave all your vegetables in a sunny place, and check every day to see what happens.

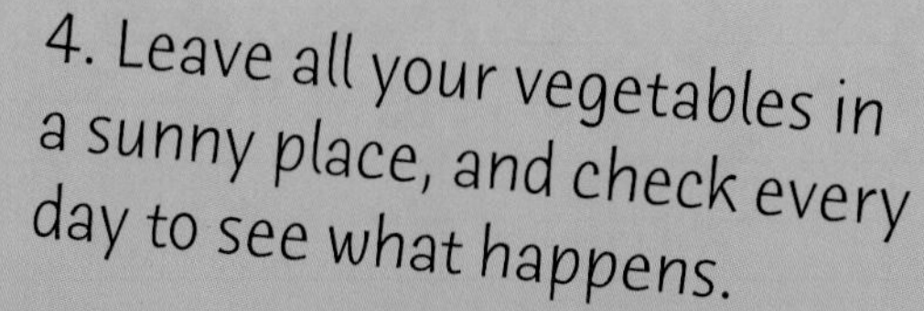

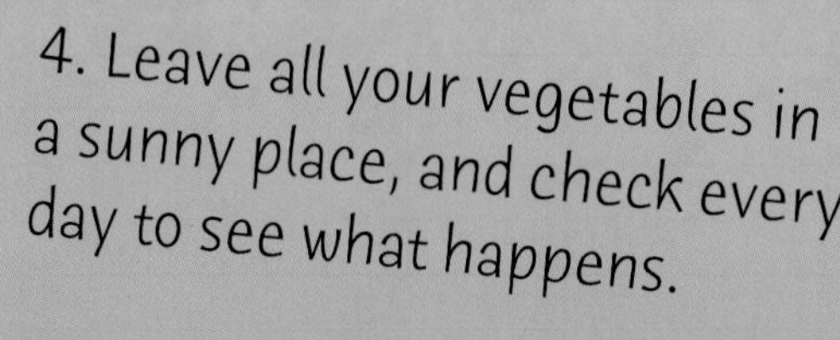

WHAT'S GOING ON?

Many vegetables are the root, bulb or seed part of the plant they come from. These parts can start to grow into a new plant. Look at the various ways they start to sprout out new plant parts. Non-organic ones may be slower to sprout, as they are sometimes sprayed with chemicals to stop them from sprouting in your fridge.

You can plant a well-sprouted potato in a tub of compost, water it, and keep covering the shoots with more soil as they grow. Eventually you'll have a potato plant and lots more potatoes!

TROUBLESHOOTER

Mark the organic vegetables with labels or a pen, so you can tell them from the non-organic vegetables.

The sprouting parts on a potato are called 'eyes'.

WHAT NEXT?

If you have any home-grown vegetables, try them too.

Black bag balloon

Make a simple black bin bag grow and float! For this to work well, you need to do it outdoors, on a hot, sunny day.

YOU WILL NEED

1) A large black bin bag, as lightweight as possible
2) Strong sewing thread

Here's What to Do...

1. Open up your bin bag and shake it out to almost fill it with air.

2. Tie the opening tightly closed, and tie on a long piece of thread.

3. Take the bag out into bright sunshine and tie the other end of the thread to something secure, like a bench or railings.

4. Wait for the bag to warm up. What happens?

WHAT'S GOING ON?

Most substances expand, or grow, as they get warmer. The sun heats up the bag and this warms the air inside. As it gets hotter, the air molecules move around more, and push away from each other harder, taking up more space. The air in the bag is now less dense than the cooler air around it, and the bag starts to float upwards. Black absorbs more sunlight than other colours, which helps warm the bag.

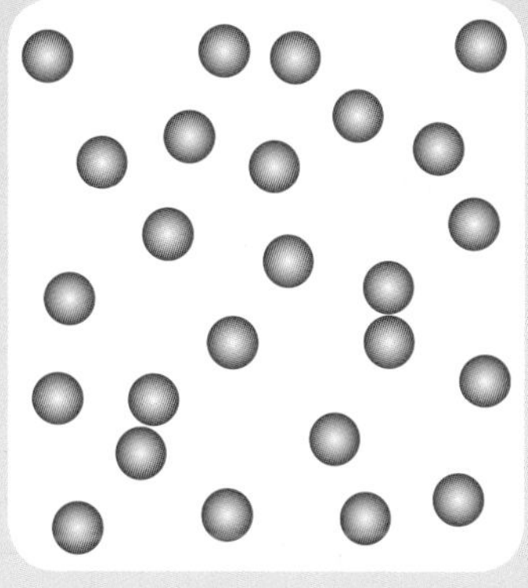

Warm air

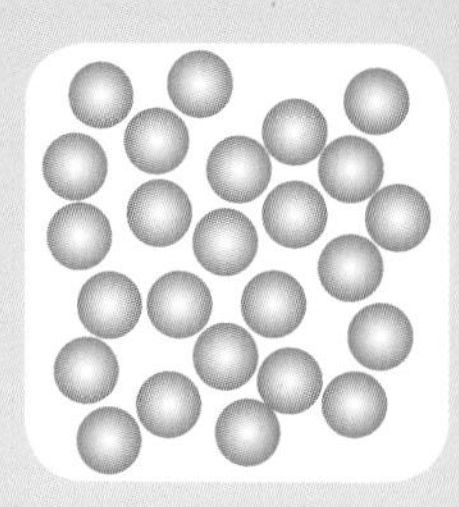

Cold air

HEAT IS MOVEMENT

As a substance gets hotter, it takes in energy. The extra energy makes the molecules move about more and faster. That's what heat is!

A hot-air balloon works in exactly the same way.

TROUBLESHOOTER

If you don't have warm sunshine, you can do the experiment indoors and heat up the bag with a hairdryer. Ask an adult to help.

WHAT NEXT?

You can buy even bigger flying black balloons, often called solar balloons, in toy shops. Or you could try making a bigger one by taping several bin bags together into a long sausage.

Make a thermometer

Heat can make things expand, so thermometers can measure heat by measuring how much things grow. This simple bottle thermometer is easy to make.

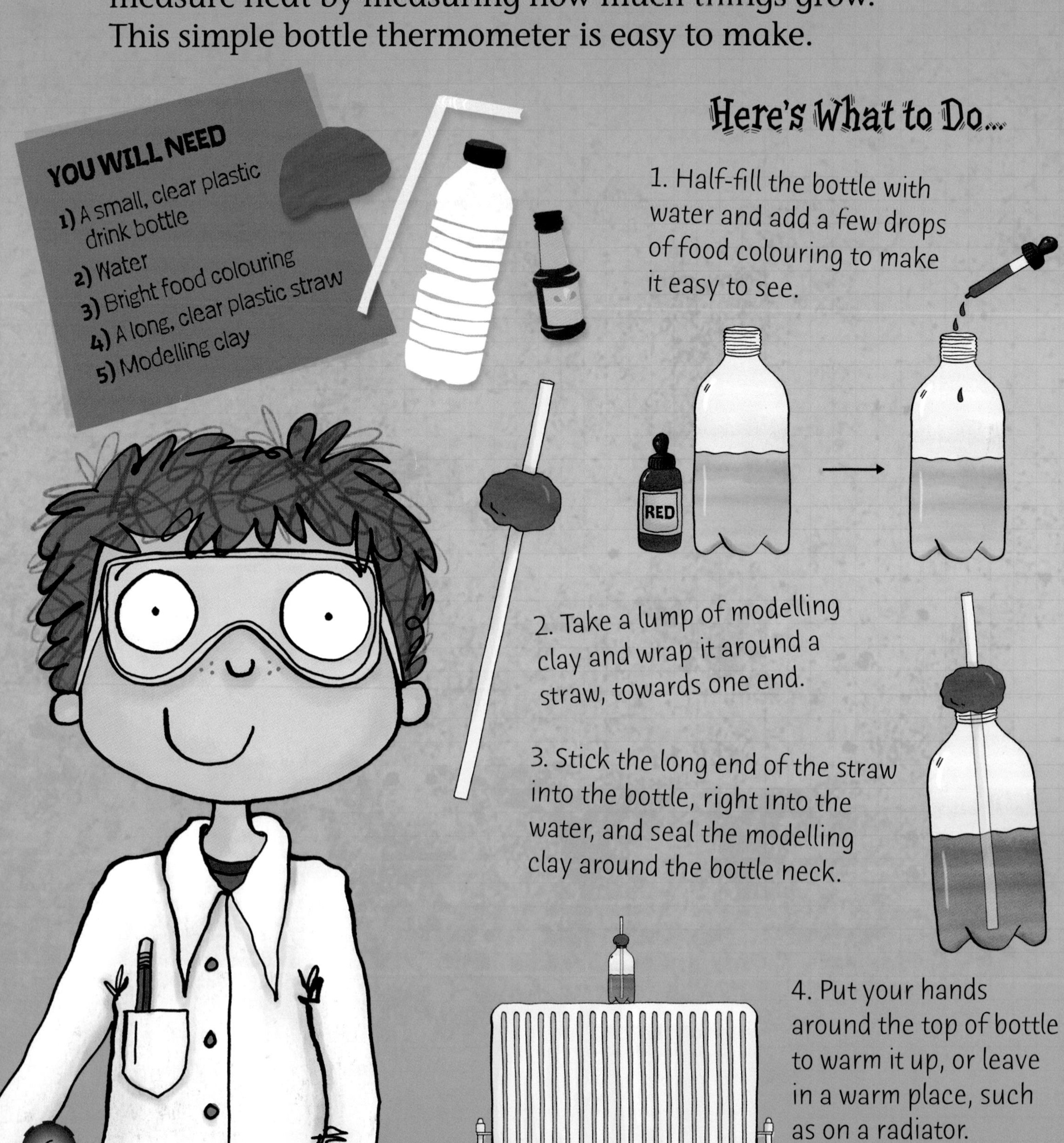

YOU WILL NEED

1) A small, clear plastic drink bottle
2) Water
3) Bright food colouring
4) A long, clear plastic straw
5) Modelling clay

Here's What to Do...

1. Half-fill the bottle with water and add a few drops of food colouring to make it easy to see.

2. Take a lump of modelling clay and wrap it around a straw, towards one end.

3. Stick the long end of the straw into the bottle, right into the water, and seal the modelling clay around the bottle neck.

4. Put your hands around the top of bottle to warm it up, or leave in a warm place, such as on a radiator.

WHAT'S GOING ON?

As you warm the bottle, the air inside it warms up and expands. This pushes the liquid inside the bottle down, and it rises up inside the straw. If you let the bottle cool down, the level will fall again.

TROUBLESHOOTER

The modelling clay must be tightly sealed around the bottle and the straw with no gaps.

EVERYTHING EXPANDS

The liquid in the bottle also expands as it warms up, but this is hard to see because liquids don't expand as much as gases do. This thermometer uses a liquid that is sensitive to temperature changes and a very thin tube, so that you can see the change in liquid level easily.

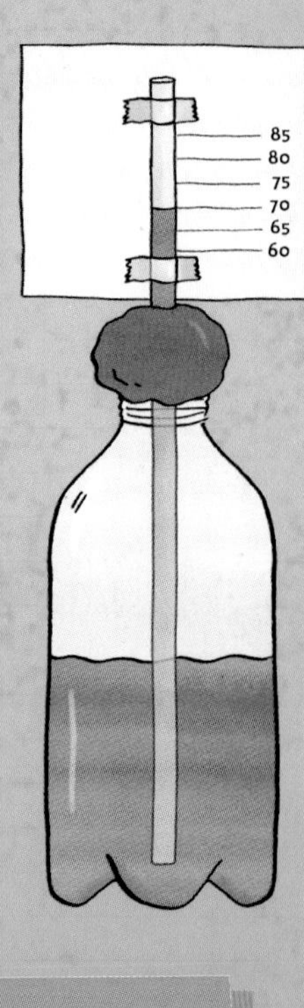

WHAT NEXT?

Tape a small piece of card to the straw, so you can mark on a temperature scale for different levels. You could use an existing thermometer to measure the temperature indoors and outdoors, then mark these levels on your own version.

Expanding ice

Most substances expand when they get warmer, and shrink, or contract, when they get cooler. When water freezes, though, something different happens – because water is actually very unusual.

YOU WILL NEED

1) Two small plastic drink bottles
2) Water
3) A fridge-freezer

Here's What to Do...

1. Carefully fill both bottles with cold water right to the brim. Don't put the lids on.

2. Stand one bottle in the fridge, and the other one in the freezer, and leave them overnight.

3. Check them in the morning. What's happened?

WHAT'S GOING ON?

When water freezes, it gets colder, so you would expect it to shrink. Actually, it expands and gets bigger, making it poke out of the top of the bottle. This happens because as liquid water becomes solid ice, the molecules form a fixed grid or lattice pattern. This pushes them away from each other, so the ice takes up more space.

Icebergs and ice cubes float because they take up more space than water, and weigh less for their size.

TROUBLESHOOTER

The bottles must be completely upright. If this is tricky, stand them on a flat, hard surface like a chopping board.

WHAT NEXT?

Take an ice cube and float it in a small bowl of water. Top up the water in the bowl until it's full to the brim. Let the ice melt. What will happen? Although the ice sticks up out of the water to start with, it doesn't make the bowl overflow when it melts, because the water contracts back to its previous size.

Sugary strings

Some substances will grow into regular-shaped crystals if they have a chance. You can make these crystal strings from sugar. Take care, and ask an adult to do the cooking for you.

YOU WILL NEED

1) A saucepan
2) Water
3) A measuring cup
4) Caster sugar
5) A wooden spoon
6) A pencil
7) String
8) Scissors
9) A clear, clean glass jam jar

Here's What to Do...

1. Ask an adult to boil two cupfuls of water in a saucepan.

2. When it's boiling, they should gradually stir in four cups of caster sugar until it disappears.

3. Leave the mixture to cool in a safe place for about an hour.

4. Tie a piece of clean string around a pencil, wet the string, and roll it in a little extra sugar.

5. Fill the jar with your cooled sugar solution.

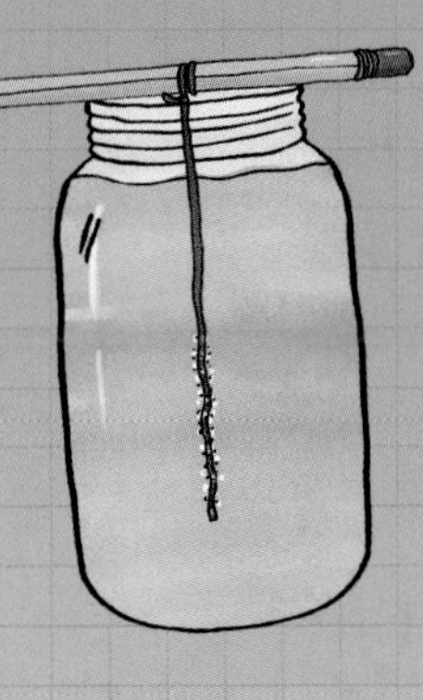

6. Place the pencil over the jar so the string dangles into the liquid. Leave in a safe, cool place for a few days.

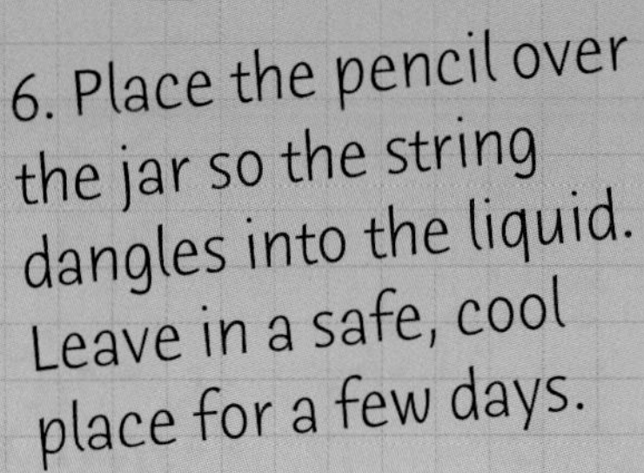

WHAT'S GOING ON?

Slowly, sugar crystals should start to grow on your string. If you leave it a full week, you should have a large clump of crystals on the string when you lift it out. Crystals form as a substance dissolved in a liquid finds a surface to stick to, and more and more of it attaches itself to the surface.

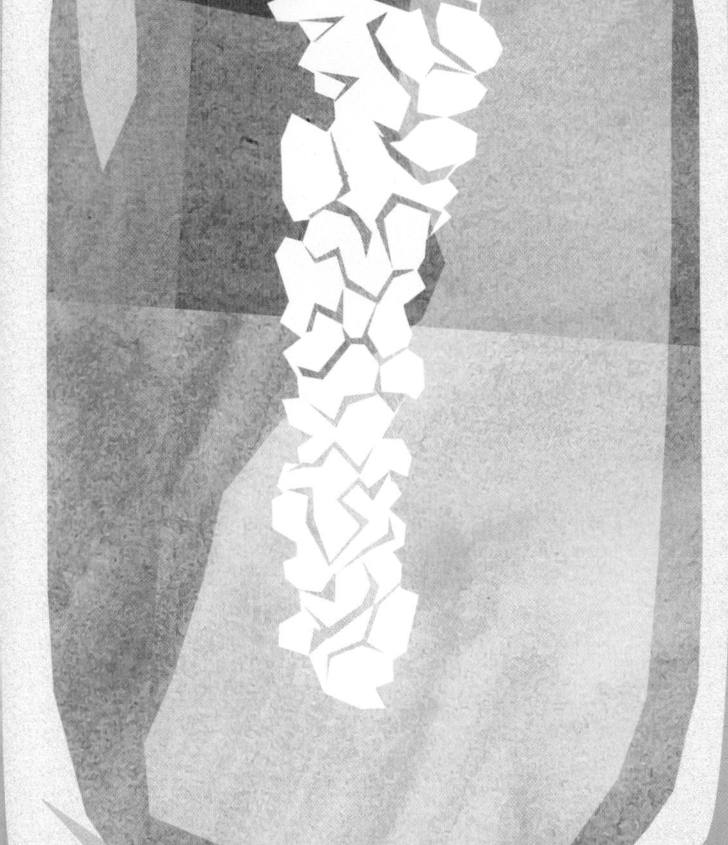

CRYSTALS IN NATURE

Many substances naturally form crystals, including sugar and salt, and various types of precious stone.

WHAT NEXT?

Make coloured crystals by stirring in a few drops of bright food colouring into the mixture after it has cooled.

Grow your own Stalactites

Stalactites grow downwards from the ceiling inside caves, as water containing dissolved minerals drips from the roof. Here's how to make your own mini version.

YOU WILL NEED

1) Two jam jars
2) Hot tap water
3) Bicarbonate of soda
4) A teaspoon
5) Knitting wool or yarn
6) Two large paperclips
7) A saucer

Here's What to Do...

1. Fill both jars with hot tap water. Add several spoonfuls of bicarbonate of soda into each one, and stir until it dissolves.

2. Take about 120 cm of yarn and fold it into four. Twist it into a single strand, and clip a paperclip onto each end.

3. Put the two ends of the twisted yarn into the two jars of soda solution, using the clips to weigh them down.

4. Position the jars so that the yarn dips down in the middle, and put a saucer underneath the dip.

WHAT'S GOING ON?

The wool or yarn soaks up the soda solution, and it collects where the yarn is lowest and starts to drip. With each drip, a bit of the dissolved soda is left behind, and it slowly forms a column or stalactite.

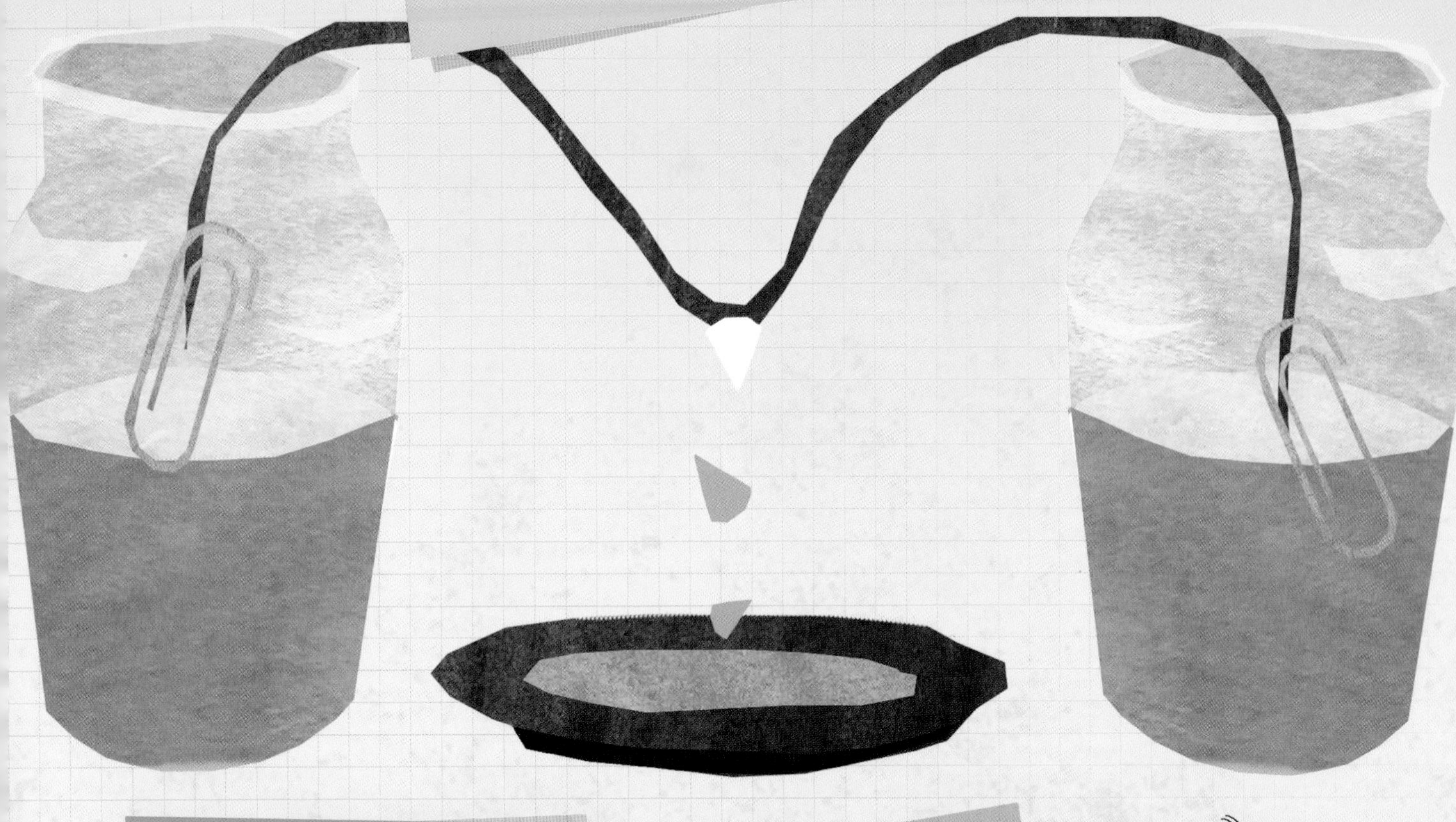

This is exactly how real cave formations grow, from limestone dissolved in rainwater – though it can take thousands of years.

WHAT NEXT?

If you leave it for a while, you may get a stalagmite forming where the solution drips onto the saucer. Stalagmites are like stalactites, but they grow upwards from the ground.

Microwave a marshmallow

What happens if you microwave a marshmallow? Can you guess? You'll need an adult to supervise, and make sure you don't cook the marshmallow for too long.

YOU WILL NEED

1) Marshmallows
2) A flat microwaveable plate
3) A microwave oven

Here's What to Do...

1. Sit a marshmallow on the plate.
2. Put it in the microwave, and heat on normal power for 10 seconds.
3. If not much happened, try an extra 5 or 10 seconds. Don't go above 20 seconds in all, or it could burn.
4. Compare a microwaved marshmallow with an uncooked one. How much bigger did it grow?

WHAT'S GOING ON?

A marshmallow is made of gooey sugar filled with tiny air holes – a bit like a foam cushion. When you heat it, the air in the holes expands. At the same time, the heat starts to melt and soften the sugar, making it more stretchy, and the marshmallow grows and grows.

TROUBLESHOOTER

It will work best if your marshmallow is nice and fresh out of the bag.

SAFETY WARNING

DON'T try to eat a marshmallow fresh out of the microwave – let it cool first!

YUM!

You can make a sweet snack by microwaving a marshmallow for 15–20 seconds on a small cookie, with a bit of chocolate on top.

WHAT NEXT?

What happens to the marshmallow as it cools down? (Once it's cool, you can eat it.)

Try cutting or tearing it open to see what's happened inside.

Popcorn!

Why does popcorn suddenly pop and get so much bigger when you heat it up? You'll need an adult to help you.

YOU WILL NEED

1) Popcorn kernels
2) A microwaveable plate
3) A microwave oven
4) A sewing needle

Here's What to Do...

1. Put a few popcorn kernels on the plate and put them in the microwave.

2. Switch on the power and wait for them to pop! How long do they take?

3. Now ask an adult to take some new kernels and carefully make a few holes in each one with a pin or needle.

4. Try microwaving the kernels with holes in them. What happens?

WHAT'S GOING ON?

A popcorn kernel is tightly packed with cereal and water, inside a tough skin. When you heat it, the water heats, boils and makes steam, which expands. When the pressure is strong enough – POP! – the kernel explodes and the starch expands into soft, fluffy popcorn.

If a kernel has holes in its skin, they let the steam out, so it's much harder for the popcorn to pop.

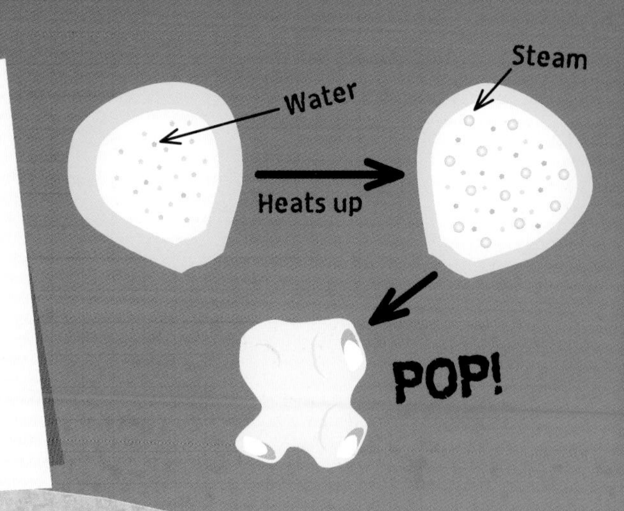

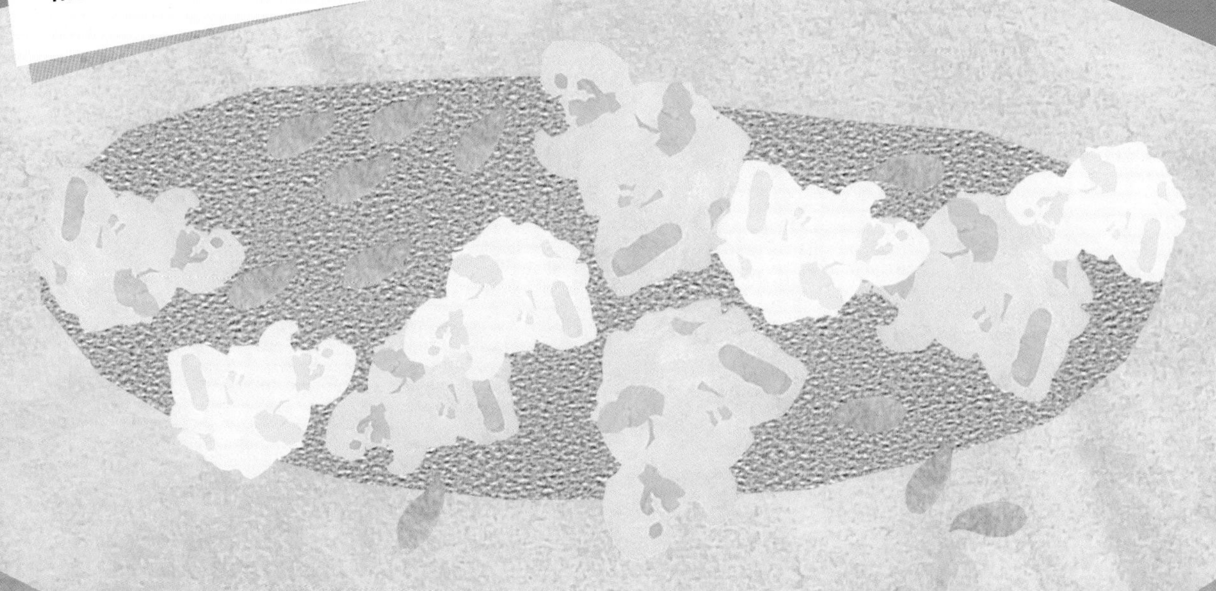

POPPED AND PUFFED

Other seeds and grains can also be popped or 'puffed' – that's how puffed rice and wheat breakfast cereals are made.

TROUBLESHOOTER

If you don't have a microwave, you can use a saucepan on a stove with a little oil in it.

WHAT NEXT?

Can you film popcorn popping and slow it down to see what happens?

Make bread rise

Look closely at a slice of bread, and you'll see it's full of little squashy bubbles. How do they get in there? To find out, try making some bread yourself.

YOU WILL NEED

1) A large mixing bowl
2) A wooden spoon
3) A teaspoon
4) A clean worktop
5) A baking tray
6) Clingfilm
7) An oven
8) 500g bread flour (also called 'strong' flour), plus a bit extra
9) Half a teaspoon of dried yeast
10) A teaspoon of salt
11) Olive or sunflower oil
12) 300ml warm water
13) An adult to help you

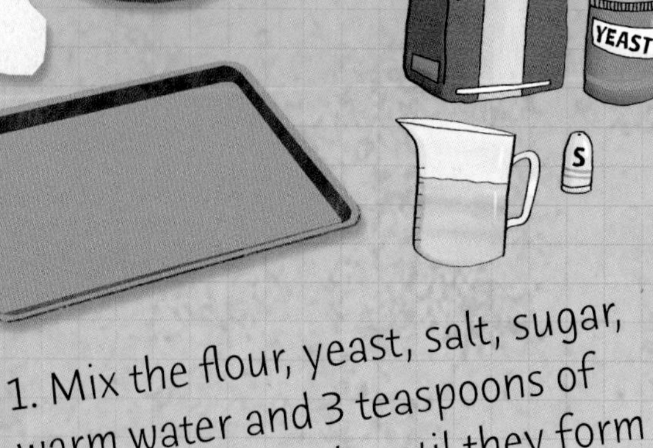

1. Mix the flour, yeast, salt, sugar, warm water and 3 teaspoons of oil in a large bowl, until they form a sticky dough.

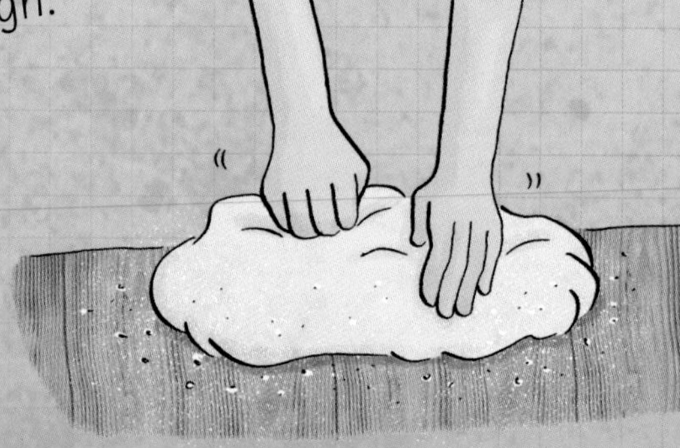

2. Sprinkle some extra flour on the table, and tip the dough onto it. Knead the dough with your hands by folding it, squashing it down, and turning it around, for about 10 minutes.

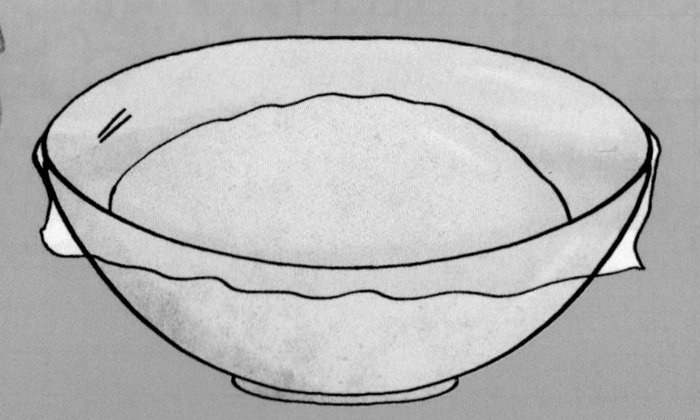

3. Put the dough back in the bowl, cover it with clingfilm, and leave it somewhere safe and warm.

4. After an hour, it should be much bigger! Take it out, knead it again, then form it into small rolls or other shapes.

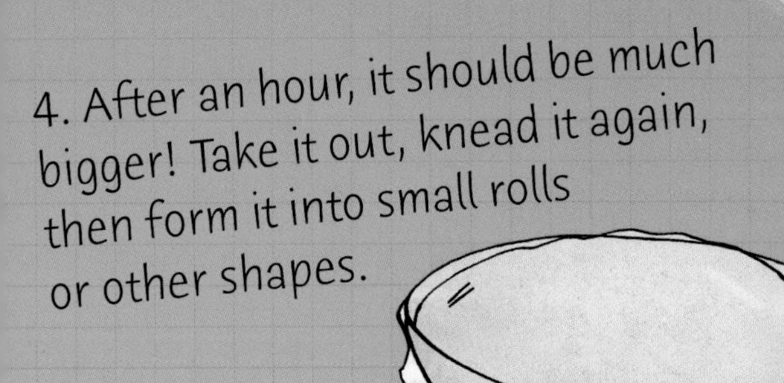

WHAT'S GOING ON?

The dough grows, or 'rises', because of the yeast. Yeast is a fungus, a living thing related to mushrooms. If it has water, sugar and warmth, the yeast cells multiply and grow, and give out carbon dioxide gas. The gas bubbles get trapped and expand inside the dough, making it rise.

5. Rub the baking tray with a little oil and put your bread shapes on it, widely spaced out. Leave them for another hour.

6. They will have grown again! Now you can ask an adult to bake them in a hot oven, at 200°C/400°F/Gas Mark 6, for about 10 minutes. Leave them to cool before eating.

TROUBLESHOOTER

The water, and the place you leave the dough, should be of a medium heat, not very hot or very cold.

WHAT NEXT?

Try making a small amount of dough with no yeast in it to see what happens.

Squirty cream challenge

Your challenge is to create a pile of squirty cream that's bigger than the squirty cream can! On your marks, get set.... GO!

WHAT'S GOING ON?

How can more cream come out of the can than was in the can? A squirty cream can contains normal, runny liquid cream, mixed with a gas, nitrous oxide. When it's in the can, the gas is held under pressure – it's squeezed together and doesn't take up much space. But as soon as it escapes from the can, the gas expands, making bubbles and creating thick, foamy whipped cream. In fact, if you squirted all the cream out, it would grow to at least three times the size of the can.

TROUBLESHOOTER

Remember the can will only squirt well when held completely upside down.

This shaving foam works the same way but you can't eat it!

FRUIT SALAD

If you don't want your cream to go to waste, do this experiment after dinner, then eat the cream with fresh fruit salad for pudding.

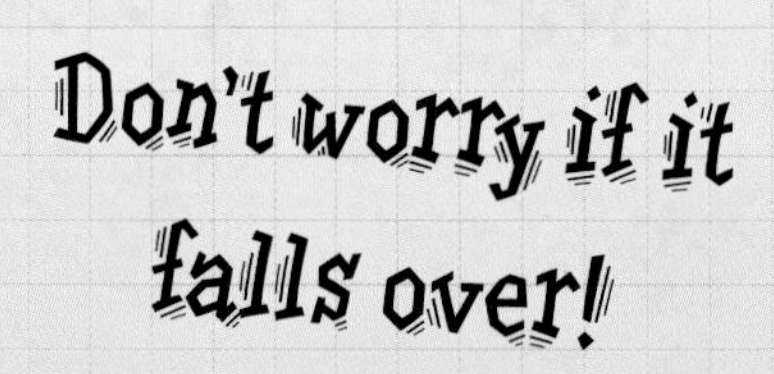

Don't worry if it falls over!

WHAT NEXT?

If you can resist eating your cream, wait several minutes and see what happens to it. You could even video it and speed it up afterwards. Does it get smaller again?

Glossary (A-C)

A

acid A type of chemical that can eat away at other materials if it is concentrated enough.
alkali A type of chemical.
amplify To make a sound louder.
amusia Inability to make sense of music.
anemometer A machine for measuring wind speed.
atoms Tiny units that substances are made of.

B

beam A line of light travelling forwards through space.
blacklight A light or lamp that gives out ultraviolet light.

C

calcium A mineral found in bones and in some rocks.
camera obscura A dark room or box with a hole that lets in light beams to form an image inside.
carbon dioxide A type of gas which is present in air.
cartilage A bendy material that makes up part of the skeleton.

Glossary (C-E)

Celsius A scale for measuring temperature.
cohesion Pulling or sticking together.
compressed Squashed into a small space.
condense To change from a gas into a liquid.
contact force A force that works on something it is touching.
contract To get smaller.
copper A type of metal.
crystal A solid substance with a naturally regular shape.

D

decibel (dB) Unit used to measure how loud a sound is.
density How heavy a substance is compared to the space it takes up.
density column A set of different liquids floating on top of each other.
dissolve To become mixed into a liquid and broken down into tiny parts.
droplet A tiny drop of liquid.

E

ear defenders Ear covers for blocking out loud sounds.
earplugs Small plugs that fit inside the ears to block out sounds.
echo Sound that has hit a surface and bounced off it.
emulsion A substance made of a liquid with droplets of another substance in it.
energy The power to do work or make things happen.
evaporate To change from a liquid into a gas.
expand To get bigger.

Glossary (F–M)

F

flexible Another word for bendy.
force A push or pull that makes things move, stop or change shape.
force at a distance A force that works over a distance or empty space.
friction Gripping force between two surfaces that are rubbing together.
fungi A group of living things that includes moulds and mushrooms.

G

gas A substance in which molecules float around freely.
germinate To start to sprout and grow.
gravity A pulling force between objects.

H

Hertz (Hz) Unit used to measure pitch, or how high or low a sound is.

L

lattice A grid-like structure with spaces in between.
lever A bar that can move up and down on a pivot, like a see-saw.
light source Something that light shines out of.
limestone A type of rock that often forms caves.
liquid A state of matter in which a substance can flow and splash.
litmus test A test that uses colours to show whether a substance is acid or alkali.

M

maglev A type of train that uses magnetic force to float above its track.
malachite A green coating made of copper and oxygen.
mass The amount of material an object contains, causing it to have weight.

Glossary (M-P)

mineral A naturally existing, pure, solid substance.
molecules Groups of atoms that make up substances.

N

nitrous oxide A type of gas.
non-Newtonian fluid A liquid that doesn't behave in a normal way.

O

oil slick Spilt oil floating on the surface of the sea.
optical fibre A bendy tube made of glass.
orbit To circle around another object.
organic Grown without using artificial fertilizers or chemical sprays.
oxygen A type of gas found in the air.

P

perfect pitch Ability to recognize and name musical notes by their sound.
pinna The sticking-out part of the ear that you can see.
pitch How high or low a sound is.
pivot A point that a lever or other machine part moves around.

Glossary (P–S)

phosphorescent Able to soak up light energy, then glow for some time.
plankton Tiny plants and animals found in seawater.
poles The two ends or sides of a magnet.

R

ray A line of light travelling forwards through space.
reflect To bounce off a surface.
refraction The way light bends when it moves from one clear substance into another.
repel To push away.

S

saliva Another name for spit.
Solar System Our Sun and the planets and moons that orbit around it.
solid A state of matter in which a substance keeps its shape.
sound waves Patterns of sound vibrations that spread out through a substance.
soundproofing Muffling sound to stop it from spreading.
spores Tiny seed-like parts released by fungi.

Glossary (S–W)

stalactite Rock formation shaped like a pillar hanging from a cave ceiling.
stalagmite Rock formation shaped like a pillar rising from a cave floor.
states of matter The forms that a substance can take: solid, liquid and gas.
surface tension The way molecules on the surface of water pull together and seem like a skin.

T

taste buds Tiny sense organs in the tongue that detect tastes.
transparent See-through, or able to let light through.
trebuchet A medieval machine for shooting at castles.
triboluminescence Sparks of light given off by some substances when they break or tear.

U

ultraviolet (UV) light A type of high-energy light that humans can't see.

V

vibrate To shake very quickly to and fro.
vocal cords or vocal folds Bands of muscle in the throat that vibrate to make voice sounds.
volume How loud or quiet a sound is.

W

water vapour Water in the form of a gas.

further reading

SCIENCE OF SOUND

Moving up with Science – Sound
by Peter Riley, Franklin Watts, 2015

Mind Webs – Light and Sound
by Anna Claybourne, Wayland, 2014

SCIENCE OF FORCES

Moving up with Science – Forces and Magnets
by Peter Riley, Franklin Watts, 2015

Mind Webs – Forces and Motion
by Anna Claybourne, Wayland, 2014

SCIENCE OF LIGHT

Mind Webs – Light and Sound
by Anna Claybourne, Wayland, 2014

Moving up with Science – Light
by Peter Riley, Franklin Watts, 2015

further reading

HOW THINGS CHANGE

Moving up with Science – States of Matter
by Peter Riley, Franklin Watts, 2015

Mindwebs – Materials
by Anna Claybourne, Wayland, 2014

The Kids' Book of Everyday Science
by Kelly Doudna, Wayland, 2014

Science Experiments That Fly and Move
by Kristi Lewandowski, Capstone Press, 2011

The Science in: A Loaf of Bread
by Andrew Solway, Franklin Watts, 2008

Mindwebs -Living Things
by Anna Claybourne, Wayland, 2014

Useful websites

SCIENCE OF SOUND

Zoom Science: Sound
http://pbskids.org/zoom/activities/sci/#sound

Neuroscience for Kids: Hearing Experiments
http://faculty.washington.edu/chudler/chhearing.html

SCIENCE OF FORCES

Zoom Science: Forces
http://pbskids.org/zoom/activities/sci/#forcesenergy

ScienceKids: Forces in Action
http://www.sciencekids.co.nz/gamesactivities/forcesinaction.html

SCIENCE OF LIGHT

Science Kids: Light
www.sciencekids.co.nz/light.html

Optics for Kids
www.optics4kids.org/home/

Useful websites

HOW THINGS CHANGE

Zoom Science: Chemistry
pbskids.org/zoom/activities/sci/#chemistry

BBC Bitesize: Material Science
http://www.bbc.co.uk/bitesize/ks2/science/materials/

SCIENCE OF LIQUIDS

Water Science for Kids
http://www.sciencekids.co.nz/water.html

BBC Science Melting Activity
http://bbc.co.uk/schools/scienceclips/ages/8_9/solid_liquids.shtml

HOW THINGS GROW

Exploratorium Science of Cooking: Bread
http://www.exploratorium.edu/cooking/bread/index.html

BrainPop: Crystals
http://www.brainpop.com/science/theearthsystem/crystals/preview.weml

Index (A-D)

Index (E-L)

Index (L-R)

Index (R-U)

Index (V-Z)

This paperback edition published in 2016
First published in Great Britain in 2015 by Wayland

Editors: Julia Adams and Annabel Stones
Designer: Anthony Hannant (LittleRedAnt)
Illustrator (step-by-steps): Kimberley Scott
Illustrator (incidentals and final crafts): Venetia Dean
Proofreader and Indexer: Camilla Lloyd

Picture acknowledgements:
All photographs: Shutterstock, except:
p. 25: iStockphoto; p. 49: Mark Williamson/Science Photo Library; p. 51: NASA; p. 63: Phil Degginger/Alamy; p. 89: Sam Ogden/Science Photo Library; p. 133 (bottom): NASA/DVIDS Hub; p. 147 (bottom): AlejandroLinaresGarcia/Wikipedia.

ISBN 978 0 7502 9782 0
Library eBook ISBN 978 0 7502 9375 4
10 9 8 7 6 5 4 3 2 1

Wayland, an imprint of Hachette Children's Group
Part of Hodder & Stoughton
Carmelite House
50 Victoria Embankment
London EC4Y 0DZ

An Hachette UK Company
www.hachette.co.uk
www.hachettechildrens.co.uk

Printed and bound in Malaysia